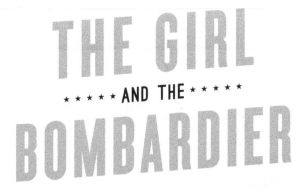

THE GIRL
★ ★ ★ ★ ★ AND THE ★ ★ ★ ★ ★
BOMBARDIER

SUSAN TATE ANKENY

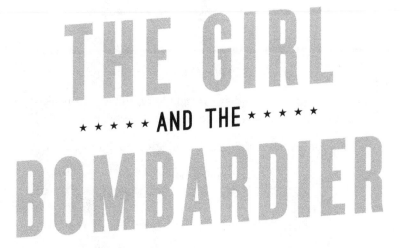

THE GIRL
★ ★ ★ ★ ★ AND THE ★ ★ ★ ★ ★
BOMBARDIER

A TRUE STORY OF
RESISTANCE AND RESCUE
IN NAZI-OCCUPIED FRANCE

DIVERSION
BOOKS

For more information, email info@diversionbooks.com

Diversion Books
A division of Diversion Publishing Corp.

www.diversionbooks.com

First Diversion Books edition, September 2020
Paperback ISBN: 978-1-63576-717-9
eBook ISBN: 978-1-63576-714-8

Printed in The United States of America

Library of Congress cataloging-in-publication data is available on file.

Dedicated to the memory of Godelieve Van Laere Pena, René Loiseau, Margot Di Giacomo, André Duval, and all the French patriots who hid Allied airmen and guided them home.

CONTENTS

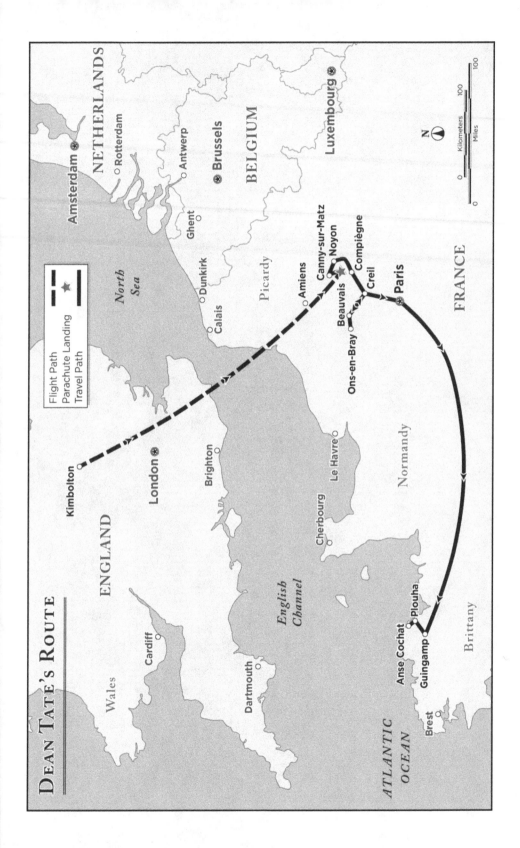

DEAN TATE'S ROUTE

Flight Path
Parachute Landing
Travel Path

ENGLAND

Wales
Cardiff
Dartmouth

NETHERLANDS
Amsterdam
Rotterdam

Antwerp
Ghent
Brussels
BELGIUM

Luxembourg

North Sea

Kimbolton
London
Brighton

Calais
Dunkirk
Amiens
Picardy
Canny-sur-Matz
Noyon
Compiègne
Beauvais
Creil
Ons-en-Bray
Paris

English Channel

Le Havre
Cherbourg

Normandy

FRANCE

ATLANTIC OCEAN

Brest
Anse Cochat
Plouha
Guingamp
Brittany

N

Kilometers   100
Miles   100

ONE

From fifteen thousand feet, the young bombardier could have seen the French countryside waiting below, but he never looked down. He closed his eyes and clung to the ledge above the open escape hatch. A steep dive had failed to extinguish the wing fires. The B-17 was going down. Crouched beside him was the navigator. Neither had parachuted out of an airplane before. "Why practice what you have to do perfectly the first time?" the smug training officer had explained. With feigned bravado, the bombardier smiled at his crewmate who yelled to be heard above the thunder of the remaining two engines still powering the plane, "Good luck, Lieutenant Tate."

The top turret gunner jumped into the compartment, and

behind him—only his feet and lower legs visible—was most likely the copilot. It was time. Lieutenant Dean Tate sat down and pushed himself from the plane. The cold struck like a bullet. He looked down expecting to see blood, and found instead glaring up at him from his chest pack the word Bottom.

Panic seized him. After an eternity of several heartbeats, he remembered a parachutist he'd met saying a chute would work upside down, but the release cord would be on the user's left instead of right. Knowing he should free-fall longer to speed his descent and avoid being caught in machine gun crossfire, but afraid the upside-down chute wouldn't open on the first try, he grabbed the metal ring and pulled. A white cloud unfurled above him.

Exhaling, he looked up. A German Ju 88 headed straight toward him. With the parachute open, he didn't seem to be losing any altitude; an easy target. The pilot flew over his parachute, causing him to swing underneath like a pendulum. He watched the German circle back and come in again. The engines grew more determined, the plane picking up speed. Dean focused on the twin propellers spinning closer. He felt no hatred for the German pilot, believing he probably didn't want to be here either, fighting someone else's war. Then the plane flew close enough for Dean to see the pilot's face. The German raised his hand and waved.

A Messerschmitt 110 crossed the sky, and Dean knew Nazi soldiers would be waiting on the ground to arrest him. They were probably watching him now. Absorbed by the German escort fighter, the ground rose up quickly below him.

Slamming onto the frozen earth back-first, intense pain like an electrical shock told him he was alive. Unable to breathe, the sky became a white blanket suffocating him. A voice in his head commanded, *Get up! Hide!*

Struggling to disengage the parachute with fingers numb

from the cold, he wondered what had happened to his gloves. Once released, he untangled himself and stood on unsteady legs. An ancient church materialized not more than thirty feet away; its stained-glass windows glowed benevolently in the muted midday light.

Excited voices floated into the churchyard from beyond a hedge. There wasn't time to hide his chute. He staggered toward the church. Someone grabbed his arm and asked in a whisper, "Deutsch?"

"American," he said, before everything went dark.

NOVEMBER 2003
PORTLAND, OREGON

I had heard the story about Dad being shot down over France so often I knew it by heart. Or at least I thought I did. Tears streamed from his eyes every time he got to the part where the cockpit window was covered in blood and the pilot's eye hung down on his cheek. After World War II, nobody talked about combat stress, and few veterans suffering from psychiatric problems received any treatment. Most were given rest, exercise, and occupational therapy, if they were given anything at all, left to endure nightmares they kept to themselves. Dad's generation accepted its duty both while fighting the war and when returning to their lives after it ended, doing what they had to do to forget. Who could blame them? While most men never talked about their war experiences, my dad told his story of being rescued by the French Resistance to anyone who would listen.

He became a father late in life, after spending years in and out of hospitals due to back surgeries and crippling arthritis. He lavished me with his time and attention. Dad had an unlimited capacity to enjoy the world. I adored him. After he retired, I tried persuading him to return to France. Over the years, the people who had helped him escape wrote letters filled with gratitude for what they called his help in their liberation and invited him to visit. But my dad never did anything for himself. He said he wanted to leave me a legacy; his happiness came from knowing he would leave everything he had worked hard for in his lifetime to me, his only child. I wondered for the first time if the reason he never returned to France might not be that simple.

Now, the unthinkable had happened: he was gone. Mom had slipped out to lie down, leaving me cross-legged on the floor surrounded by cuff links, tie clips, and neatly folded cardigans patiently awaiting their fate. I lifted a lifeless gray sweater and inhaled, hoping for cherry vanilla tobacco, finding instead the stale, chemical scent that always hung in the nursing home.

Beside me were two boxes, both on the verge of disintegrating with age. One contained Dad's air force uniform, and inside the other I found neat stacks of envelopes, black-and-white photographs, and loose notebook paper covered in Dad's delicate, cursive script. From a Manila envelope I pulled his typed memoir, the title neatly centered on the cover page: A Tribute to a Gallant Few. Rummaging deeper, I found mission reports, bombing records, dog tags, and the fake identity cards he used to travel by train in France.

There were letters from people whose names I knew as well as my own: André Duval, René Loiseau, Margot Di Giacomo, Jacques du Pac, and Godelieve Van Laere. The names were so familiar I had forgotten these people were French Resistance members who fought and risked their lives for the liberation of their country and for the lives of Americans like my father. I lifted a bundle of faded pink envelopes bound together by a thick rubber band.

Lassigny, France
Saturday January 17, 1945

Dear Lieutenant Tate,

I wait a long time before writing. I have learn English and only after many months I feel able to write a letter. I hope you remember me, I am the blond Belgian girl with whom you got acquainted in February 1944 on a Saturday night. My name is Godelieve Van Laere. My family will be please to receive some news from you. In a letter which you sent to Capt. Edelston you told that you were an instructor now. Why you are not a parachute instructor? You jump very well!

In the last winter my brother and me, we went in the AAF (army), but after 8 months I was tired of the soldier's life and I be back home now. I am understanding better how dangerous it is to be a soldier and I am very thankful towards every body of the air force who helped us in the fight for our liberty. I send this letter to your home because I believe you are in the Pacific theater of operations.

I look forward a letter and please tell us about your health. Accept the best greeting from my father, mother and brother. My sister is still in Germany. The Germans discovered her job.

Good luck in your next missions and God bless you.

Sincerely friend,
Godelieve Van Laere

There were other letters from Godelieve, the most recent dated 1994. Even if she were still alive, it seemed unlikely I'd find her at the same address. But, "What if?"

The idea refused to be extinguished. I could learn more about Dad's time in France, all the details I had ignored and taken for granted, and the pieces of the story I never knew.

My research would enable me to remain connected to him, to keep him alive, and maybe replace my grief with something constructive. I wanted to tell these people who rescued my dad that his life had been worth saving.

Leaning against the bed my parents had shared for sixty-three years, I smiled at the final gift from my dad, the box with his story waiting to be discovered; a story of ordinary people doing extraordinary things.

I wrote to Godelieve and didn't hear back. Regretting not having maintained some contact with her during Dad's long years of decline, and devastated at the lost opportunity, I resigned myself to never knowing.

There were enough leads in the box to keep me busy for months, if not years. I contacted the organizations Dad had belonged to, like the 8th Air Force Historical Society of Oregon and AFEES, the Air Force Escape and Evasion Society. I began to look for the others who had helped my dad, and it didn't take long to find them. I was put in touch with a man in France, Dominique Lecomte, who has made it his mission to reunite Allied evaders and their families with the "helpers" who had hidden them. He invited me to a commemoration ceremony for a crew shot down the same day as my dad's. Some of the people who helped Dad would be there.

One day, a letter arrived from Laucourt, France.

23 February 2010

Dear Suzan,

I received your letter and I thank you very much. I am sorry to hear your parents past. It is always very hard to lose father and mother. I remember when we visited them at San Francisco your mother was so proud of you and how much they loved you. Your father was very tired and your mother told us he had a stroke some months ago. We thought they were very courageous to make the trip. I was very happy to see the lieutenant I met on 8 February 1944. He was still the same. I will try to give you the information you need to write the story of your father. I have the journal I kept during the war. But I remember your father and our time together like he was here only yesterday.

On the 50th Anniversary of D-Day in 1994 I was in Normandy. The weather was very bad, almost the same as 1944. I saw a veteran and he looked so lonely. I went to him and said this bad weather makes you remember the horrible day. He came to me and his eyes were full with tears. He said, "I lost all my best friends." Never I'll forget that poor man and never can we forget the sacrifice from the American people. I think it's our duty to inform the young people in Europe and even in the States how courageous and generous has been America. It was for us a great honor to help your courageous boys. The 8 February was a very bad day for the American air force and we felt bad when a plane crashed. It was for our liberty but for you American people it was a tragic sacrifice. We can never pay our debt. It was our duty to help your boys and we will never forget. We have to honor your people and remember forever your courage and generosity. Every war leaves bad memories and sacrifices. Your letter brings fraternity. May your story be an example in future for peace for every country.

Godelieve Van Laere Pena

TWO

THE END OF A DREAM

In December 1941, Dean was a senior at Pacific College in Newberg, Oregon. He'd been accepted to law school and hoped by some miracle to avoid the war. As an attorney, he planned to give a voice to the poor and downtrodden, far away from his claustrophobic small town and elderly, if well-meaning, parents. His dream crumbled when a draft noticed arrived a month after Imperial Japanese forces attacked Pearl Harbor.

Dean was born on April 7, 1920, in Portland, Oregon, to Will and Tracie Tate who lived in the working-class community of St. Johns. Waiting for Dean at home was his four-year-old brother, Wayne. The first years of Dean's life were spent moving as his dad searched for a way to support his family.

In 1926, Will and Tracie bought a gas station in the center of Silverton, Oregon, and turned it into a restaurant. Business limped along in those Depression years, never making the kind of money necessary to do more than just survive. While Dean's parents spent all their waking hours at the restaurant, he learned to take care of himself. Pressed by his family's tight finances to pick hops and sell newspapers when he was six years old, he quickly grew resourceful and independent.

Facing bankruptcy, Will sold the restaurant in 1934, and the Tates moved to Newberg, a small town about thirty miles northwest of Silverton. Will, ashamed of what he considered his own failure, suffered bouts of depressive illnesses until landing a job as an independent mail carrier. Tracie took seasonal jobs whenever she could, picking cherries or shelling filberts. June mornings often found the entire family picking cherries.

At Newberg High School, Dean became driven to escape the hand-to-mouth existence his parents lived. He did well in athletics and academics, working seven days a week at Nap's Grocery Store to save up for college. He spent late nights studying instead of sleeping in hopes of earning a scholarship to Pacific College in Newberg.

Quakers founded Pacific College in 1885. Also called the Society of Friends, Quakers did not believe in killing another human being for any reason. When drafted they registered as conscientious objectors, serving at desk jobs or assisting the wounded on the front lines, and never carrying firearms. Influenced by discussions in his college classes, Dean agreed that peaceful dialogue could be a means to avoid armed combat. War wasted lives, and with a dubious outcome; World War I was supposed to have been the war to end all wars.

The draft ordered Dean to report for induction in May, a month before his graduation. When his request for a deferment was denied, the college president sympathized and allowed him to submit his thesis and take final exams early to receive his degree, but the law school acceptance he had worked so hard to obtain had to be turned down: a bitter pill to swallow.

According to his brother, Wayne, whose request to enlist had been denied without explanation, the Navy was the best way to go—no hand-to-hand combat or planes shot from the sky. But Dean couldn't swim and, in fact, hated water. If he had to go to war, and apparently, he did, he wanted to learn to fly a B-17.

Dean had been interested in airplanes since he flew in a biplane when he was eight years old. His dad had given a traveling demonstration pilot a free meal in exchange for taking his son on a ride. Soaring over Abiqua Creek, the Gallon House covered bridge and the orchards where he picked hops, the weightless sensation of flight soothed him, and with the pilot behind him and out of sight, he imagined he was flying the plane alone. This was what freedom felt like, he thought. There wasn't another soul around to bother him, nobody telling him what to do.

By 1942, everyone was taken in by the glamour and romanticism surrounding the men who flew the B-17 bombers. Movie newsreels showing a formation crossing the Channel into occupied France to bomb a Nazi munitions plant looked like an advertisement for a fun-filled vacation. The Flying Fortresses paraded along runways, and then, an assembled crew of handsome warriors in uniforms posed beside their noble steed. A young airman flashed a smile over his shoulder before climbing into his plane. Dean imagined himself a pilot, a knight in a heavy sheepskin jacket going forth to do battle against the forces of evil. If he had to give up law school, maybe flying wouldn't be too bad.

On May 16, 1942, Dean, in the backseat of the family's chestnut-colored sedan, watched the rising sun wink between the upturned arms of Douglas fir trees on his way to Portland where he would be inducted into the United States Army Air Corps. He pressed his head back against the leather seat and thought about his dad who had stayed home. Seeing his son off to war was too much for the frail old man.

An hour ago on the front porch, Dean had tried to reassure him. "It's all going to turn out okay, Pop, and I'll be home before you know it. By the time I finish my training, the war will probably be over." The old man's hands shook as he pulled his son into an embrace. Five feet two inches tall, with a few wispy strands of white hair tossed about his round head, he looked much older than his fifty-five years. Dean briefly wondered if they'd ever see each other again.

His father kissed him and, stepping back, pulled a handkerchief from his pocket to wipe the tears streaming down his cheeks. "Good luck, son. Take good care of yourself."

"I will. And take care of Scotty for me." The Scottish terrier at their feet tilted her head at the sound of her name and stared up at them.

The idea that he was going off to war filled Dean with a deep despair, and despite what he told his dad, he didn't expect to survive. He worried, if he didn't return, would his parents' lives be lost as well?

The Governor Hotel in downtown Portland was now home to the army induction headquarters. Under the black awning and spreading along the sidewalk, a crowd of young men, parents, girlfriends, wives, and children tearfully said their goodbyes. Dean turned to his brother, dressed in baggy clothes, his arm tossed around his wife's shoulders. He had always been the picture of brotherly watchfulness and responsibility, and Dean was filled with affection for him.

"Come back soon, Pub," Wayne told him, using his childhood nickname. "We'll be waiting."

Dean hugged Wayne and his wife, Reola, and then bent to his mother. She wrapped her arms around his shoulders, gathering his shirt into her fists, not caring about wrinkling the fabric she had ironed several times last night. He kissed her cheek, picked up his bag, and turned away. She stood with her eyes fixed on the door long after her son had disappeared into the building.

A week later, Dean arrived at Sheppard Field Air Force Base outside Wichita Falls, Texas, as lightning skittered across a sky laden with heavy clouds. He had never been farther from home than the Oregon Coast, and now, three thousand miles from Newberg, and a stranger for the first time in his life, he experienced a deep loneliness. He found the other cadets, also away from home for the first time and not optimistic about their futures, were cautious with friendly overtures.

Tracie Tate dumped chopped rhubarb into a saucepan and carried it to the stove where a comforting green apple scent rose up from a batch of blood-red jam waiting to be poured into jars. Returning to the sink to scrub the last batch of rhubarb she opened the window, inhaling the fresh-cut grass and grape-scented lilacs. At this moment, when the intoxicating air held the promise of spring, the war seemed far away. Footsteps on the front porch interrupted her thoughts, and she rushed through the living room toward the entryway where the mailman had already deposited several letters through the slot. Scooping the mail from the floor, she found an envelope with Dean's graceful handwriting. Sitting on the first step, she tore it open and read:

May 29, 1942

Dear Mom and Pop,

I'm in Wichita Falls, Texas, a God-forsaken place: hot and dry. It's already too hot in the early mornings when we're outside for exercises. The lightning is incredible and continues all night long. I've never seen anything like it. The land is flat with hardly any trees so you can see for miles in every direction. I was told the army got the land for this airbase from a cattleman for one dollar. They got robbed.

After I left Portland, I went to Fort Lewis, Washington for my official induction. I took several tests including a mental evaluation. At my physical I was 5'6" and 135 pounds. I was given some shots, a bad haircut, and new clothes. I'm sure you've received my "civilian" clothes by now. I wish I could have kept them so I could feel like myself once in a while.

I passed the exam to become an aviation cadet. At the end of basic training in December, I'll take the test to qualify for pilot training.

Give my regards to everyone. I'll call you when I can.

Love, Dean

Dean wrote to his parents daily in the beginning. The letters he received from family and friends became a lifeline that made the early months of cadet training less lonely and almost bearable.

June 10, 1942

Dear Dean,

The commencement ceremony at Pacific was very nice. You were missed. Your classmates left a vacant chair for you. The president, Mr. Gulley, in his address to the graduates, spoke so kindly about you, mentioning the excellent leadership you provided as class president and of course you and Bill winning the tennis championship, and then he asked me to come forward and accept your diploma. And I had to walk right past your empty chair and not cry. I was strong even though my trembling chin threatened to betray me.

Many people came up to us and wished you well. Bill thinks he will be called up soon. His parents brought us over some peaches and sweet peas. Hazel Mary came to dinner last night.

I hope the slippers I'm sending will be what you need. I'll send some cherries soon. We miss you. We know you're working hard and we are proud of you.

Love, Mom and Pop

In December, Dean missed the score needed for pilot training by a single point. His friend Tony Zaladonis earned the same score, and both were recommended for bombardier training. Tony said, "We'll get to drop bombs. How hard can that be?" Bombardiers had a better survival rate than pilots, someone told him. The statistics told a different story. In a study of battle casualties in the 8th Air Corps from June to August 1944, 16 percent of bombardiers were killed. The only position in the B-17 with more deaths was the waist gunners at 19 percent. Seven percent of pilots died in battle. The findings showed the bombardier, with the most critical job, also occupied one of the most dangerous positions, unprotected from bullets and flak by the Plexiglas nose.

Dean and Tony were transferred to Ellington Field, about fifteen miles southeast of Houston, for the Bombardier Cadet twelve-week flight school program. Dean possessed many qualities necessary to make an effective bombardier, such as the ability to remain calm under pressure, good judgment and independent thinking abilities, and a methodical attention to detail; what he lacked was motivation. He wasn't willing to risk his life for a war across the world that hadn't affected him personally.

Two weeks after Dean's graduation and officer commissioning, he spent four weeks at gunnery training in Wendover, Utah. He participated in stationary target practice and learned to clean and load a machine gun and a forty-five-caliber pistol, which was standard issue for officers.

Lacking enthusiasm for guns, Dean felt it was just as well when his time in Wendover was cut short. A month after arriving, Dean's crew received orders to report to Walla Walla, Washington, to complete their training. They would be needed as replacements in Europe. Five months ago, hopes for the Allied Forces in Europe had run high, but by July, the US 8th Air Corps was suffering devastating losses.

Walla Walla, in southeastern Washington State, sat in the middle of nowhere, a perfect location to practice dropping bomb loads. Although closer to Dean's home, it was still a long day's train ride to Portland—and an impossible hope that he'd be granted enough time or that his parents would be able to make the journey to visit him.

On a languid August morning fragrant with sun-drenched wheat, John Martin and his ten-member crew started training to become a coordinated team, flying together for the first time in a B-17. Dean watched Martin pull himself into the plane through the escape hatch near the front of the aircraft. It looked easy enough. After tossing his bag up into the plane, he grabbed the doorframe and pulled his legs up to his chest.

There he hung, not sure how to get the momentum to swing his legs up and through the doorway. Dean stood back and watched as the copilot lifted himself into the plane in one fluid motion. *Jump, tuck, and swing*, Dean repeated to himself. He tried again, and fell back onto the tarmac, landing in a squat. The hell with it, he thought, and walked around to the waist door on the other side of the aircraft. A B-17 had four exits, twice as many as the B-24s. The nose exit, or escape hatch as it was also called, was just outside the nose compartment where the bombardier and navigator were stationed. The tail gunner had a small door at the rear of the plane, and the waist door and bomb bay made up the other exits.

Walking through a B-17 required navigating a series of compartments and narrow passageways. Entering the waist door, Dean turned right and headed up through the cylindrical waist compartment toward the nose. This was the gunners' domain, and they were sitting on the floor laughing when Dean entered. Johnny Johnson, the right waist gunner, raised a hand in greeting. He manned one of the thirteen .50 caliber machine guns that earned the B-17 its nickname: the Flying Fortress. Nearby sat a red-headed kid named Walter Kelly, the left waist gunner, and beside him the tail gunner Jim Slick, a gregarious kid from Utah.

Dean maneuvered his way around the ball turret—manned by a small, freckle-faced boy named Bob Taylor—before stepping up into the radio room where the engineer Tom "Mac" McCaffrey worked at his desk. Seeing Dean, he smiled and said, "Something wrong with your door?"

Dean dipped his head to enter the bomb bay compartment. On each side of the catwalk, the racks where the twelve

500-pound bombs would hang were empty. Another doorway led to the area behind the cockpit where the top turret gunner, George Bishop, was stationed. Dean maneuvered his way around the turret platform where one step would take him to the pilot and copilot.

Lt. Charlie Halfen was a reserved and professional copilot, but had a youthful face that made him look as though he were playing dress-up in an officer's uniform. To Halfen's left sat pilot Lt. John Martin, a Washington, D.C., native who attended military school in Texas before graduating from Georgetown in pre-law and going on to receive an MBA in finance from Harvard. His father, Major General Frederick Martin, had commanded the Hawaiian Air Force at Pearl Harbor when the Imperial Japanese forces attacked on December 7, 1941. When Dean first met Martin, he worried that this cultured, well-educated man would think him a hick, but Martin looked down on no one.

Dean jumped through a hole into a passageway underneath the cockpit, passing the nose escape door on his left, and ducked through the final doorway into the nose compartment. The Plexiglas nose, a rounded, acrylic covering like a picture window, flooded the space with bright light. Dean passed Carl Carden bent over some figures at the navigator's desk and stepped up onto the raised platform holding the bombardier's chair. Perched on this seat, Dean experienced the sensation of being suspended in air with only Plexiglas to prevent him from falling out. He rested his feet on the transparent acrylic. The Blue Mountains appeared dark against the eastern sky, and surrounding the runway, golden blankets of wheat extended to rolling grass-covered hills.

The Norden bombsight would sit on its pedestal directly in front of his chair. The Norden was a telescopic target-tracking analog computer that looked something like a large camera and cost twice as much as the average American home. The bombsight helped the bombardier drop the bomb load accurately, allowing the US, the only country going to such lengths, to avoid civilian deaths to the greatest extent possible. The Norden was crucial to the new and controversial daylight precision bombing campaign's success. It was dangerous, some said suicidal, to drop bombs over Germany in broad daylight. The proponents claimed the Norden made it possible to drop a bomb within a hundred-foot circle from an altitude of 21,000 feet. In combat conditions it was far less accurate.

While Dean and Carl prepared for the flight in the nose compartment, above them in the cockpit Martin started the engines. Today the pilots were to practice getting the B-17s into formation, a delicate process they had practiced without their crews onboard. The goal was to assemble in the correct position and practice placing their wingtips one hundred feet, or about six cars lengths, apart. Bombers were built with large wings for stability, allowing them to fly close together. A tight formation meant security.

Throughout August, Martin's crew flew daily fixed-point bombing missions. Long days began before sunrise and finished after dark. Four times they landed to reload their bombs. After the final landing they refueled the plane and completed their other duties before going to dinner around ten-thirty.

On August 26, they flew their first night mission. The target was lit, although not well enough, and getting into formation would have proved suicidal. Abandoning the attempt, they returned to base feeling defeated as respect grew for the British Royal Air Force, who flew their missions at night.

The American 8th Air Corps and the Royal Air Force joined together in a campaign called the "Round the Clock

Offensive." The Americans bombed Germany and occupied countries during the day, and the British bombed them at night. The losses to the 8th Air Corps had become tremendous, and it was argued that daylight precision bombing should be abandoned. But the Air Corps clung to its belief that daylight bombing would be the secret to winning the war with better accuracy and fewer civilian deaths than nighttime raids.

When Dean and his crew received their final orders, Dean had only trained for three months, nine months fewer than the required year, and had logged one hundred and eighty-one flying hours, far fewer than the Air Corps recommended for flight officers to be capable of flying across the Atlantic and into battle.

FROM SCOTTFIELD, ILL
SEPTEMBER 27, 1943

SPECIAL MOVEMENT ORDERS OF HEAVY BOMB CREWS.
ORDERED TO GO PRESQUE ISLE, MAINE, REPORT
TO CO FOR FURTHER ORDERS SUBSEQUENT TO
MOVEMENT OVERSEAS. REPORT TO STATION 117.

A week later, John Martin, copilot Charlie Halfen, navigator Carl Carden, and bombardier Dean Tate departed Illinois in a new B-17G to cross the Atlantic Ocean on what was called the "Snowball Route," a series of refueling hops through Goose Bay, Labrador, Greenland, and Iceland. The first stop was Bangor, Maine. John Martin wrote in his journal on October 7, 1943:

Beautiful country with trees all turning yellow and red. Lots of lakes with no roads leading in. Prior to reaching Goose Bay over Gulf of St. Lawrence ran into snow—a first! Looked like someone wrapped the ship in a blanket of white. Went on instruments for two hours. No radio reception, hence no weather reports. Broke out ten minutes out from Goose Bay and flew contact over to the field—thanks to pretty fair navigation. Landed in the dark, still a novelty, with usual two bounces. Before we could eat we were briefed on our next flight to Greenland, Bluie West 1 "the toughest little field in the world."

The briefing was nothing more than photos and a short movie about the difficult landing, and directions to find the correct fjord, in the dark, on southwest Greenland's coast. After locating the correct fjord, marked by a wrecked freighter, Martin would have to fly inland up the fjord with mountainous walls of several thousand feet on either side. "All fjords look alike and you can't back up an airplane, so you better do it right the first time," the briefer told them.

John Martin spent a day at the Goose Bay airfield working on engine number two, which had been giving him trouble. The crew took off that night at two a.m. To everyone's relief, the flight to Bluie West proved uneventful. After refueling and eating a hot meal, the crew departed for Iceland. Almost immediately after taking off, one engine stopped and another began to act as though it might give up as well. Less confident than he admitted, Martin began the trek across the ice cap at the low elevation of 1500 feet in case they encountered difficulty. Martin wrote, "We bared on until dawn over a damnably cold stretch of water. Icebergs went floating by and I swear I saw polar bears playing on one."

Martin and Halfen, distracted by an ailing engine, became lost somewhere between Greenland and Iceland. Carl and Dean tried desperately to get a fix on their location using the stars, or celestial navigation, but the movement of the plane was too erratic to hold the sextant steady. A low-fuel light meant Dean and Carl had twenty minutes to find land or end up in the icy water. Halfen broke radio silence and called for help. There was no response. Dean scanned the blackness for any sign of land. Carl reviewed maps, speed, and heading, and suggested they change course. Within minutes the radio compass picked up a signal. The crew had been heading out to the open waters of the Atlantic.

Between 1943 and 1945, four hundred bomber crews were lost en route to their stations, most due to pilot inexperience.

Their final stop for refueling before reaching England was Ireland. The sobering experience across the Atlantic took nine days and erased any romantic sense of adventure they'd had when they left the States.

Dean's first sight of Kimbolton airfield was not what he expected. Circling the station, bombers were visible scattered along the central runway and its tributaries like abandoned toys. Upon landing, they passed a bomber riddled with holes, and from its nose, missing the Plexiglas shield, the bombardier's instruments hung out, still tethered, as if caught in their attempt to escape. Dean searched and found no signs of life. Had the station been attacked or abandoned? A hollow, gut-wrenching dread replaced the elation at surviving the Atlantic crossing. He wasn't supposed to be here. This was a terrible mistake, a nightmare become too real.

Martin, Halfen, Carden, and Tate reported to headquarters. A humorless commanding officer told them how to find their squadron's living quarters. Stations in England were spread out—dispersed bases were harder to destroy with one well-placed bomb. They walked in a murky drizzle for what seemed like miles along muddy roads rutted with puddles. Finally, just as it looked like they were going into the woods, they found the Nissen hut that would be their home. "Let's go have a drink," Martin said as soon as they'd seen their rooms and dropped their bags.

The officers' club resided in an aluminum, arched-roof Nissen hut alongside other nearly identical structures not far from the flagpole and message board where a sign read: *Welcome to Kimbolton, home of the 379th Bombardment Group.* As Martin and his flight officers entered, the men assembled at tables around the room stopped talking. Pale, haunted faces stared at the replacements as if they were ghosts. In the background, a radio babbled an upbeat tune incongruous to the ominous mood.

At the bar, covered in a red and white-striped awning, Martin and his men ordered drinks before settling around an unoccupied table. Two pilots approached and Martin smiled and stood to shake their hands. The men did not smile back. The taller one weaved slightly from side to side as if standing on a ship's deck in a rough sea. An empty pipe hung from the other man's mouth.

As the pilots pulled up chairs, Martin asked, "What happened here?"

The tall one, named Tom, said, "This outfit was pretty shot up yesterday, another raid to Schweinfurt, Germany. I think it's over. There aren't enough planes left or men to fly them." His hand shook as he brought his glass to his mouth.

Schweinfurt was deep in Germany, a long route for bombers, and home to three ball-bearing factories. The 379th had been there in July, and no one had wanted to go back when yesterday Colonel Preston read to the assembled crews the same message read at all stations around England participating in this mission:

Operation send in clear. This air operation today is the most important air operation yet conducted in this war. The target must be destroyed. It is of vital importance to the enemy. Your friends and comrades that have been lost and that will be lost today are depending on you. Their sacrifice must not be in vain. Good luck, good shooting, and good bombing.

The Teletype message had been tapped by the Germans, and the Luftwaffe waited in full force. Six hundred men died, over a hundred of them from Kimbolton, on the day history would rename Black Thursday, and October 14, 1943, would be remembered as the day with the largest losses for the Air Corps during all of World War II.

Dean returned to his room knowing it wasn't good fortune that landed him a room to himself. He pressed down on the bed and found, instead of a mattress, three thin, damp foam pads. He might as well be a prisoner.

THREE

GERMANY

John Martin's crew flew their first mission five weeks after arriving, and without Dean. The doctor, who had prescribed something for Dean's cough, grounded him for three days. The base was experiencing an epidemic of colds, and in some cases, pneumonia. With no hot water, the men were told to avoid showering because the doctors believed it was contributing to the illnesses. Hot showers were available at the Red Cross in Bedford twenty miles south. For the most part, the men resigned themselves to being dirty.

Dean thought he was well enough to fly. Martin didn't want to take the chance and go against orders. Besides, Martin told him, "You can make up the mission by asking to be assigned to another crew as a substitute bombardier." That didn't sound too difficult. Martin's crew flew to Norway on a mission that turned out to be a "milk run," as the men called easy missions.

A week later on the day after Thanksgiving, Dean flew his first mission, a virgin among crewmates who believed they were seasoned after the Norway run. Sitting in the back of a six-by-six truck, slumped forward and half asleep, the crew cursed the cold November dampness and the early hour. Their cigarettes made tiny red arcs in the darkness as their disembodied voices rose out of the shadows. "Where is the God-damn driver?" "What's holding us up?" "Let's get this show on the road."

Briefings were dramatic events, but an airman's first was especially terrifying. Dean hoped his first mission would be anywhere but Germany—Norway, maybe, or even France. Up front, a black curtain served as backdrop behind a stage. The air smelled of leather, tobacco, and unwashed bodies, as the men who had entered loudly in nervous expectation now quieted down. The show was about to begin.

Someone in the back shouted, "Ten hut!" and the men rose to their feet as Colonel Moe Preston walked briskly up the center aisle radiating confidence. Stepping onto the stage he looked like a giant, tall and broad, with thick, blond hair neatly groomed away from his square face. Dipping his head, he said, "At ease, gentlemen."

A West Point graduate born in Weed, California, Preston arrived at Kimbolton station when it became operational six months prior in May of 1943. In the first months, he lost 75 percent of his original crew, and no single target was bombed well enough to disrupt German manufacturing. Despite Preston's promise to court-martial any crew that aborted a mission, crews disappeared to sanctuary in neutral Sweden or Switzerland.

When lists were posted for an impending raid, crewmembers failed to show up for briefing, sometimes turning up in sickbay with symptoms Preston suspected were psychosomatic. Each airman knew that he was unlikely to survive beyond eleven missions and any given mission could be his last. Trained to keep a distance between himself and his men, Preston knew emotional attachment caused a commander to be less effective. Despite his aloofness, he was popular with the men at Kimbolton station.

The colonel made a few warm-up remarks before two wooden doors near the stage were pulled open to reveal a map. The men groaned. Yarn marked a course across the North Sea to Bremen, Germany. Dean's empty stomach clenched; he'd been too nervous to eat any breakfast. Ignoring the sounds of complaints, Preston continued. The target would be a plant where Focke-Wulf 190 fighter planes were made outside the city of Bremen near the port area. Red splotches marked the areas where the men could expect heavy flak, and where they could expect a greeting from around five hundred bandits or more. Dean's hands began to shake at the mention of bandits, an innocent-sounding nickname for German fighters. In a drawing of the formation, Dean found their plane, relieved to see it was in an inner, more protected position.

Colonel Preston ended the briefing with, "Keep tucked in, and don't allow your formation to become stretched out. The sacrifices that will be made today are necessary for us to win this war. Your work will not be in vain. Good luck, and good bombing."

Someone in the back yelled, "And goodbye!" Dean stood in stunned silence for a moment before he realized the men around him were leaving.

Martin and the crew gathered under a wing of their B-17

they had named *The Old Fox*, the nickname John Martin had earned for being able to talk himself or any member of his crew out of trouble. Looking up from his papers, he saw Dean coming across the runway holding a short-handled black bag containing the top piece of the Norden—the football, it was called. In the other hand, he carried a zippered cloth case with tools and instruments needed for the mission. Martin smiled at the sight. The guard looked like he was escorting a child to his first mission.

At five minutes past eight they were on their way to Germany. One after another the B-17 bombers rose into a sky beginning to color with dawn. Within seventeen minutes, all eighteen aircraft leaving Kimbolton station were airborne. At twenty-three other bases around eastern and central England, a similar scene played out as aircraft took flight for the day's mission.

Entering Europe, black puffs from anti-aircraft guns on the ground appeared like dancing phantoms, causing the ship to tremble and rock. Flak, the name given to the ground-fired exploding shells, appeared everywhere and out of nowhere. Sitting in class, learning about daylight precision bombing, Dean had chosen to ignore an obvious fact: they would be sitting ducks. At 25,000 feet, in bright sunlight, there was nowhere to hide. Sweat dripped into his eyes. Most airmen would remember waiting for flak explosions as the worst stress they had ever known.

The flak decreased as they entered Germany's airspace, and Dean looked down on peaceful green fields. A German fighter plane appeared to come out of the sun, a gray blur darting out of sight followed by another close behind. Dean and Carl tried to shoot the fighters, but they were too fast. Dean fired his gun with a surge of adrenaline-infused strength until his arms began to ache and the triggers froze. He shook them and pushed against them to no avail as fighters continued to sweep in.

Martin, his face dripping sweat, reported engine number two inoperable. When the engine that had plagued him since Goose Bay gave up, it was usually followed by the loss of a second engine. They needed all four to keep up with the formation.

As they neared the target, small, white clouds appeared around the plane from exploding twenty-millimeter shells fired from the ground—popcorn, the smoke was called. Smoke flares indicated the lead bombardier had found the target in his bombsite. Martin said, "Okay, Bombardier, we're holding our own, it's all yours. You're flying the plane from here to the target."

"Bomb bay doors open," Dean reported. The plane rocked from side to side. He braced himself with his feet to keep his eye on the bombsite lens. "There it is," he whispered, spotting the target. "Bombs away."

As the last bomb dropped, the plane lifted upwards, freed from its burden. The ground exploded in flickering white lights and pillars of billowing smoke. Dean turned toward Carl who lifted a thumb and smiled. Mission accomplished. "Bomb doors closing," Dean said into his interphone.

Martin turned back into formation when a B-17 took a direct hit in front of them, disintegrating into fire and black smoke. There were no parachutes. Once they crossed the Channel, Mac's steady voice broke the silence over the interphone, "We're at ten thousand feet. You can take off the oxygen."

Dean lit his pipe and sucked on the stem until the shaking stopped. Smoking was not allowed in flight. He didn't care. When practicing with unmanned targets, it had been easy to ignore what he was training to do. Innocent people had been killed today. He had dropped the bombs that killed them.

With only two engines still functioning, Martin brought the bomber onto the runway with his signature two bounces, sailing past the waiting ambulance and fire truck and Colonel Preston on the tower with his binoculars still fixed on the northwestern sky. The ground crew, having watched the gray afternoon sky and pacing like expectant fathers, ran toward the bomber, bursting with relief to see their plane home safe and mostly unharmed.

The airmen jumped from the plane slapping each other's backs and laughing. "We gave 'em hell!" "We sure did!"

The eight holes in the aircraft were closely examined and the ground crew boasted they could have her fixed up and ready to go again by tomorrow. Dean's smile faded. The idea he would ever have to get back in the plane for another mission was impossible to consider.

The crew headed immediately into debriefing to answer questions as they ate sandwiches and drank coffee. Later, Martin, Halfen, Carden, and Tate went to the officers' club. They knew the dark secret they didn't understand this morning: they were expendable.

FOUR

"SOMETIMES, DEAN, I WONDER WHAT IT'S ALL ABOUT"

Dean's second Christmas away from home was approaching without fanfare. He avoided the officers' club, having grown tired of the morbid bragging about how many Germans had been shot down after a mission, even though he understood this was how men handled their fear. At times he experienced a depressed sense of loneliness, unable to tell his parents and friends the truth about where he was or what he was doing—that he was always cold, it rained constantly, mud was their real enemy, and he was sick and tired of Spam and Brussels sprouts. He missed home, his family and friends, and most of all his freedom.

Days blended into one another in nameless succession as missions were scheduled and canceled due to weather conditions in Germany, often at the last minute with bombers and their crews lined up on the runways, or worse, after the crews had waited on the runway for hours.

Dean suffered a severe reprimanding each time he missed the designated target. Despite his familiarity with being in trouble for disregarding rules, the episodes demoralized him. Before being commissioned, he would have fought back with some comment like, "Do you think I'm missing the targets on purpose? Because if that's true, you have a much bigger problem on your hands." Arguing wouldn't do him any good, and above all else he needed to control his impulses so he could complete his twenty-five missions and go home. At this rate it might take years instead of months. Waiting and never knowing became an emotional test of endurance.

A letter from his mother brought the news that his dog Scotty had been poisoned. He couldn't imagine why anyone would want to harm her. He remembered arriving home on leave and whistling for her from the bus station.

DEAN TATE'S JOURNAL
DECEMBER 16, 1943

Bad weather in Germany gave our crew a two-week break. Today we flew our fourth mission; all of them have been to Bremen where the target was submarine pens. I read in The Stars and Stripes *that we're being used as bait to lure the Luftwaffe out of hiding. We expected as much, but it was pretty rough to see it in print. Two months ago when I arrived here I saw myself as a knight going to battle against the forces of evil. Now I'm beginning to wonder if I'm not more like Don Quixote. Instead of a gladiator in a flight suit, I see myself as a fall guy, trying to patch up what the politician's can't, or won't. But I'm not sure we're doing anything of any use to anybody.*

Death has never bothered me particularly. Even in the very thickest of battle I maintain an aloofness from death and the thoughts of its possible consequences. When my buddies fail to return from a mission, I'm heart-broken and disconsolate. But I never believe that some Boche 20 mm cannon might force me into a premature entrance into the cloudy mist which men are wont to speculate upon, but from which none are permitted to return. I think death is probably easy. It's the dying part that bothers me. Still, I can't shake the images. I watched a fort get its tail shot off. I saw the tin fly when it was hit. It went into a spin from 28,000 feet, all four propellers whirling. No one got out.

Colonel Preston told us that no more than 12 percent of our bombs are falling on the targets. The remaining 88 percent fall somewhere. Where? On civilians? I can't make any sense out of that.

Martin gave further impetus to my cynicism after we landed today. The flak had been thick as hell, the crew was on edge and irritable; nevertheless, we were overjoyed at being home again with nothing more serious than a couple of flak burns. Martin slapped me on the shoulder and quite casually said, "Sometimes, Dean, I wonder what it's all about." Martin is a good guy, well educated and serious minded. He has an unusually keen insight into human psychology, with all its intricate ramifications and effects, particularly upon young boys faced for the first time in their lives with death. However, he often says portentous things without comprehending the effect of his words upon others. Such an admission of doubt from one whom I considered the antithesis of doubt; one who had always seemed above and beyond cynicism was, to say the least, confusing to my already wondering mind.

The boys around the squadron all seem enamored with this same sort of cynicism. I asked my buddies, what is it we're trying to do? No one is sure. All the men I talk to just want to know that someone cares about what they're doing. I asked if any of them had a definite, concrete, logical explanation for the war. Are we fighting a crusade against tyranny and oppression? What are we fighting against? I ask pointed and blunt questions such as: Is the war really worth the price? Will peace after this war be any more successful than after the First World War? Is it our duty to clean Europe's periodically dirty pants? For the most part my interrogations avail me nothing but ridicule, and answers like, "G'wan for God's sake, pipe down, you're gettin' a second John's pay and three squares a day."

I imagine there's a danger in this type of discontent spreading. What if we all throw in the towel?

Whether we are fighting for liberty ultimately isn't important to me. However, finding someone who actually believes in our cause has become very important to me. I want at the very least someone to fight for, someone who knows positively and indubitably that our ideals are not empty mockeries. Perhaps it sounds juvenile, but if I have to risk my neck daily, I want, at least in the eyes of someone, to be a savior and a liberator; not a sucker as I'm beginning to believe I am.

Occasionally I run across a serious minded, thought-provoking chap who will spend some time telling me what he thinks. However, even the thoughtful ones fail to ignite a spark within me. I can't quite reach the point where their words, however well chosen, sound real.

One afternoon when it wasn't raining, Dean rode the bicycle he'd been issued into the village of Kimbolton. Flying down the road, inhaling the sweet, spicy scent of wet leaves, Dean felt free for the first time since his induction. He pedaled onto High Street, the main road through the village, once meant for carts on market day, and now crowded with American jeeps. The Americans' arrival had brought an overnight change to sleepy Kimbolton and its fewer than 800 inhabitants. With their big, flashy smiles and loud greetings, "Hi, there! How ya doin'?" they looked and sounded like they'd stepped out of a Hollywood movie. In the late afternoons, jeeps came plowing into the village to stop abruptly outside

the pubs. Young airmen spilled out, victorious warriors celebrating another day of successfully defying death. They were
forgiven their loud, rambunctious ways after determining
they were as harmless as overgrown children; and, after all,
they had finally stepped up and come to help England win the
war.

Without a plan or anything better to do, Dean decided to
visit the vicar he'd met one evening at the officers' club. A tall
stranger with thick, white hair and luminous blue eyes had
introduced himself as Reverend Powys Maurice of St. An-
drew's Church in Kimbolton village. They fell into easy
conversation and before the vicar departed, he patted Dean's
shoulder and invited him to visit the rectory one day soon.

Dean made his way to the thatched-roof parish house adjoining the Anglican church. The housekeeper ushered him
into a cozy sitting room where a fire blazed in an enormous
fireplace. As he held his hands toward the flames, Reverend
Powys Maurice entered the room. "Ah, you've come to see me
at last. Sit down, young man, won't you? Care for a gin and
tonic?" The gin had been a gift from a general who had recently visited the vicar.

When the old man expressed his gratitude for the lieutenant's bravery, Dean confessed, "I don't deserve any credit.
I'm not even sure what I'm doing in this war. I blame the
politicians for not being able to fix this mess and for costing
the lives of so many innocent people. I just don't think war is
the answer to the problems the world's facing."

The pastor frowned. "I am afraid young man, that you have
far too cynical an outlook. Perhaps we should shine your tar-
nished armor a bit." He smiled warmly and Dean knew that
out of respect he should keep his views to himself. "We British like our saviors to fight the good fight, but we also like
them to fight with consuming Christian zeal, and for them to

have a knowledge of the principles for which they are fighting." The vicar walked over to the fire and jabbed at a log
with an iron stoker. "You American airmen have an admirable
disregard for death."

Dean shook his head and put down his empty glass. "To be
honest with you, I didn't want to fight this war; in fact, I consider myself a pacifist. I think there are better ways to solve
problems than killing each other. All I want to do is survive
by some miracle and go home."

The vicar regarded him with bright eyes. "What church
were you raised in?"

"Methodist. My parents and my brother are religious. It
didn't rub off on me. I'm a bit of a misfit in my family." To
some of the airmen, home became a religion, a sacred place
they would do anything to get back to, a thing worth fighting
for, and a destination greater than heaven. Dean admired
their faith.

Dean continued, "I can't reconcile my belief in God with
what's happening. And, I'm not even sure what we're fighting
for or against."

The vicar turned from the fire to the bombardier. "Young
man, we're fighting for our very existence; not for some ideal;
not to make the world safe; not even against tyranny and oppression. No, Lieutenant, we are not fighting a 'politician's'
war. We're fighting to live as Englishmen, as Christians, and
as gentlemen. God does not ask you to fight for Him. He asks
you to fight for your fellow man. That's your purpose and
your ultimate glory, to help others who desperately need your
help."

The vicar returned to his chair. "If we can die with our
hearts and minds fixed on attaining an honorable goal, knowing we have lived out our purpose regardless of our personal
success or failure, then we have lived a life that matters."

On New Year's Eve, Dean and the radio engineer on his crew, Mac, ended up in London at a bar off Piccadilly Circus called the Honky-Tonk, where hostesses who weren't above prostitution served cheap beer and a cigarette-smoking piano player beat American tunes from a broken-down piano. Intending to create an American atmosphere, it fell pathetically short. They'd been given unexpected leave for New Year's Eve, unaware of the reason for it. Bombing raids were going to increase in January. This would be their last freedom for a long time.

Dean and Mac had hit it off right away when they first met in Walla Walla. Two distinct groups existed among airmen: officers and enlisted men. Dean didn't fit into either. He felt inferior to other officers, who were mostly college educated and from families with money. The enlisted men, mostly from hard-working families like his own, were trained to not fraternize with officers. Mac didn't seem to care.

Dean watched Mac lead a platinum blonde hostess around the tiny dance floor. A tall, stocky kid with quick-witted charm, and a curly lock of thick brown hair over his right eyebrow, he was equipped with limitless energy and had been an all-around athlete in high school before enlisting to serve his country. After the war he hoped to become a police officer like his father back in New Rochelle, New York. Dean thought his humble, non-judgmental selflessness and his ability to find the best in every situation would serve him well. The crew loved him for his natural ability to make light of any news, no matter how depressing. Dean noticed that Mac didn't report when he saw a plane go down during a battle, bucking protocol because he was unwilling to dispirit the other crewmembers.

A hostess asked if he wanted another pint. She'd been by twice and both times he'd refused. This time he accepted the offer despite his dislike of beer. There was no gin or whiskey to be had outside the officers' club back on base. Usually she wouldn't have appealed to him; her experience was the kind he lacked, but there seemed to be something about her, something he couldn't name or pull himself away from.

He and Mac, both virgins, were curious about the unknown intricacies involved in sex. When it came to romance, Dean's attempts had mostly fallen short with the girls back home. He dated and had a few girlfriends, like Hazel Mary, but nothing serious. He had been more focused on school than finding a wife. After being commissioned, he learned women behaved differently toward a man in uniform. It was like slipping into a new identity.

Returning with a beer, the hostess asked in a teasing tone why he wasn't wearing any medals. Since coming over in October he'd earned an air medal for flying five missions, a bronze medallion with a diving eagle clasping a lightning bolt in its talons. "Everybody in the Air Corps earns medals," he told her. "All you have to do is climb into the plane and return alive, or not, actually. They're meant to make you feel important. And if you feel important, maybe you'll keep fighting. It doesn't mean that much to me." Taking a sip from his glass, he resisted an impulse to cringe.

"It means something to me," she said. He wasn't the hero she wanted him to be. He got in the plane to do his bit, as the British called it. He believed himself a coward.

One by one the customers disappeared, and she slipped into a chair at his table. She was eager to talk, and he learned she was born and raised in Cardiff where her father managed a pub. On January 2, 1941, the place was packed with mill workers, miners, and ship-builders celebrating the break in the bombing raids. They hoped the worst was behind them and Hitler had finally realized the British would never surrender. It never occurred to them the sudden clearing in the weather might give the Nazis an opportunity the weather had stolen.

The screaming air-raid sirens tore through the streets and alleys. Maybe the customers in the pub didn't hear the aircraft in the distance or they ignored the sirens, sick to death of being enslaved by them, raising a fist to the "dirty Huns" before ordering another pint. After the bomb hit, forty-two bodies lay mangled and torn apart, indistinguishably entwined with floorboards and chairs and each other.

She returned home that night to find the place her family had worked and lived was gone; her dad, mother, and younger sister blown to pieces. Her eight-year-old brother and his friends had been coming home from a church party when the sirens began and they were ushered into the local baker's basement. The next morning, children gathered outside the bakery to stare in innocent fascination as the bodies that had been their friends only yesterday were removed from the debris. Among the dead was her brother.

She wiped at the tears on her cheeks with the base of her thumb. Dean took a drink and shifted in his seat to hide his discomfort. She leaned in and kissed him, melting against him. When she pulled away, Dean thought he saw something in her eyes that hadn't been there before, and later he would wonder if he'd imagined it.

He didn't sleep with her. Instead, he left her all the money he had with him. Later, he told Mac he didn't want to become part of the gonorrhea epidemic plaguing London on his first try. The truth was it seemed wrong. He promised himself to make each mission a crusade for the Welsh hostess.

FIVE

SHOT DOWN

Dean woke to pounding on his door. "Lieutenant Tate. Briefing in one hour." He flipped on the light and squinted at the clock—four a.m. Only an hour had passed since he went to bed. Martin's crew hadn't been scheduled to fly today, and he'd forgotten to check the status board for his name listed as a substitute bombardier. Tempted to stay in bed, he swore at the cold virus that grounded him, causing him to fall behind his crew. If he didn't show up for briefing, he'd earn an extra mission, maybe two, and he was trying to make up, not add, missions.

Through a thick, damp fog, and a vengeful headache, Dean trudged to the mess hall hoping the mission would be scrapped so he could crawl back into bed. Fresh eggs, bacon, and pancakes piled high on his plate made his stomach rise. He wouldn't be able to eat. He never could. An enormous breakfast before every mission was well anticipated by most airmen. Dean looked at it as his last meal.

The briefing felt even more foreboding than usual without his regular crew around him, and when the operations officer pulled back a curtain revealing the target—Frankfurt, Germany—the airmen collectively muttered protests. Colonel Preston ignored them. "Gentlemen, today's target is Frankfurt. I believe you know it. The target—the same you bombed four days ago. Unsuccessfully, I might add. You can expect heavy flak, and more fighter planes than the last mission."

"And less chance of returning alive," a man sitting behind Dean muttered. A commanding officer pointed out buildings surrounding the target, including a school to avoid. Dean tried to swallow the gathering dust in his throat. Colonel Preston would be flying the lead aircraft today. Someone in the back whistled. If the colonel was coming along, this was an important mission—and a more dangerous one.

After the briefing, Dean went to the supply room where his personal items were put into a large envelope labeled with his name and home address, a reminder that today's mission could be a one-way trip. He imagined his parents being handed the envelope on their front porch and shook his head to dislodge the vision.

In the nose compartment Dean found the navigator, Eugene Gallagher. Eugene had flown with Martin's crew as a substitute on a mission to Kiel. He was a good navigator and Dean's confidence, which had deflated during the briefing, tentatively reemerged. The fog outside the aircraft remained thick, and Dean remembered the two B-17s that recently collided after takeoff in similar conditions. Everyone on board was killed. "Killed in Action," their families were told, which was partly true. It made parents and wives feel better than knowing an accident had killed their son or husband before they made it to the battle.

Dean asked about the pilot, hoping for some reassurance. Eugene told him Lieutenant Beam, "while not what you'd call friendly, was fearless and tough as nails." He had become this crew's pilot only a little over two weeks ago, and he was close to completing twenty-five missions. Dean wondered if the rumor was true about how he shot up the officers' club one night and lost his forty-five as a result.

Eugene apologized for the plane being unnamed, a fact some considered bad luck, but Dean told Eugene he wasn't the superstitious kind.

They were late joining the other bombers after fog delayed their takeoff. From England to Europe, fifteen miles across the English Channel, Beam struggled to catch up, leaving them on the outer edge of the formation. Dean and the crew knew they were exposed and vulnerable to enemy attack. The Germans were ready and waiting for the stragglers.

Entering France, the fog lifted, the sun became a blinding white orb, and all hell broke loose. A single-engine, one-manned German fighter plane, a Focke-Wulf 190, appeared straight ahead at 12 o'clock, screaming toward them, guns blinking.

By the time the copilot told the crew on the intercom to get ready, the German had fired, shooting the Plexiglas nose full of holes. Wind rushed into the nose compartment like a hurricane. Smoke blinded the bombardier and navigator. Eugene grabbed the fire extinguisher, but flames appeared everywhere and multiplied too quickly.

Outside Dean's window, flames covered the wings where the gasoline was stored. "Oxygen fire in the nose, and the wings are on fire," he reported to the pilots.

A waist gunner reported half of both the horizontal and the vertical stabilizer shot off. Beam's voice on the interphone told them engine number two had quit and number three was aflame with fires burning near the gas tanks. He plunged into a dive to try to extinguish the wing fires.

Dean and the navigator were knocked to the floor as the plane's nose headed straight for the ground. The bomber shook and screamed. Face pressed to the floor, eyes squeezed shut, Dean braced himself and begged the plane to level. The dive seemed to last too long. He wondered if something had happened to Beam, and if they were about to crash into the ground.

The plane began to level. Dean pulled himself to his chair, looked outside, and yelled into his interphone, "Fires almost out on the wings." Only silence answered him.

Dean stumbled and crawled his way to the flight deck where a stench like raw meat greeted him. The cockpit windshield and the two men flying the plane were covered in blood. From the pilot's empty eye socket the eye, still attached, hung down onto his cheek, and his shoulder oozed blood through shredded flesh and leather. Dean leaned in between the two men.

"I gave the bail out!" the pilot yelled, wrestling the yoke to keep the plane under control. "I can take her down alone." Dean didn't move. "Get the hell out of my plane! Now!" the pilot roared, shocking his bombardier into obedience. The co-pilot grabbed his parachute and turned to Beam. Briefly, the two men looked into each other's eyes. They would not see each other again.

Dean made his way back down the smoke-filled passage to the nose. "Bail out," he told Eugene, grabbing his parachute and snapping it on his chest harness. He pulled the hinge pins from the escape door and pushed. Nothing happened. He pushed again with all his weight, and the door gave way and fell from the plane. He crouched in the doorway, paralyzed with fear. Thoughts tumbled over each other. Thoughts like, could Beam land the plane with only one eye?

Outside, a giant propeller roared. With both hands he clutched the ledge over the escape door. He had never practiced bailing out, nor even been told how to do it. And now, by the dumb luck of being first to arrive, he would be the first to go.

Eugene knelt behind him, bloody and burned, and yelled, "Good luck, Lieutenant Tate." The top turret gunner jumped into the already cramped compartment. Dean sat down and pushed. As he fell, tumbling, something struck his chest. Forcing his chin down to see if he'd been shot, there on his parachute pack staring up at him was the word *Bottom*. With his left hand he grabbed the metal ring and pulled hard, releasing the parachute and slowing his descent.

Raising his head, he saw a yellow-nosed Ju 88 headed straight toward him. His body tensed in preparation for the bullets that would kill him. The pilot flew over, nearly missing the top of his parachute. Dean turned his head to watch his opponent circle back and heard the mighty twin engines grow louder. He fixed his eyes on the approaching propellers, unable to hate the pilot, believing both of them would rather be anywhere else. When the German flew close enough for the two men to see each other's faces, he waved, and flew out of sight.

Dean hung limply beneath his parachute, incredulous to be alive. His eyes were fixed on a Messerschmitt 110 circling above him when he hit the frozen earth back first.

Stunned, but alive, he disengaged his parachute and tried to stand. Airplane engines droned overhead. There were voices. He needed to hide. An old church with tall spires stood close enough to reach. He surveyed his surroundings and stumbled a few feet toward sanctuary before a man grabbed him by the arm and whispered, "Deutsch?" Dean looked over his shoulder where an old man was gathering the discarded parachute into his arms.

Dean shook his head. "American," he said and collapsed.

SIX

GODELIEVE

PICARDY, FRANCE

Seventeen-year-old Godelieve Van Laere studied the February sky outside the beauty shop window with familiar anticipation. Bombers crossed overhead like a flock of prehistoric birds moving south. The purr of their engines had become a voice of encouragement promising one day France would be free. The door flew open, swirling frigid air around the small room as Madame Dorez, the baker's wife, burst in, pointing outside with an outstretched arm. "Look! Paratroopers!"

Godelieve untied the smock from her neck and hurried to the front window, where the other women, both customers and stylists, pushed against her in their excitement. One said, "Maybe the Great Landing has begun!"

Three parachutes with human forms dangling underneath

descended against the alabaster sky. Godelieve's eyes clung to the nearest one, low in the southern sky and floating down as languidly as the first winter snowflake. Her heartbeat quickened. Everyone waited for the Allies to come and liberate France, and even as rumors circulated through the northern villages, no one knew when it would happen. Every day eyes turned to the sky, hoping paratroopers would appear to put an end to their misery under Nazi occupation.

Godelieve longed to see an American face-to-face and to look into the eyes of a real hero, someone greater than God to those waiting for freedom. Even if this was not the Great Landing and only another plane shot down, littering the countryside with lost Allied airmen, she might be able to help, if she could reach the paratrooper before the Germans. Godelieve placed the coins from her pocket into Madame's palm and ran from the shop. "But I have not dried your hair yet," Madame called after her.

From her bicycle, Godelieve called out to Monsieur Orliac, tramping along the dirt road and shrouded in baggy farm clothes. Seeing her, his weathered face broke into a toothless smile. There was nothing to fear from the old man who often spoke of seeking revenge for his son's brutal death at the hands of the Gestapo. When asked if he had seen the paratrooper, his old muzzle collapsed in on itself like a dried apple, and she feared he might go into a lengthy monologue about his ailing wife. Instead he pointed south and told her the paratrooper probably landed up the road near the next village, Plessis-de-Roye.

"Merci," she yelled over her shoulder, already pedaling away. There were no more parachutes. Three paratroopers seemed a feeble start to the Great Landing. Her spirit refused to be dampened and she pedaled faster, the cold air whipping her wet hair against her face.

A German plane dipped low to skim the barren beet field beside the road, searching for the downed airmen. Not wanting to draw attention to herself and lead the Nazis to the paratrooper, she slowed down. Fear knotted in her stomach, and she wobbled on her bicycle as her vision blurred and her head swam. She was still a child then, four years ago, when the Nazi planes flew over her family as they tried to escape the advancing German army and began firing. The terror rose fresh, as if it had happened yesterday.

In 1940 she had lived in Fresnières, a village less than an hour's walk north of Lassigny, with her mother, father, eleven-year-old brother Jan, and her nephew, baby Willy. When her older sister Clarisse wrote from Belgium telling her parents she was pregnant and uninterested in raising the child, Godelieve's father went to Belgium and brought the baby home. He and his wife would raise the little boy as their own.

Godelieve Van Laere was born November 10, 1925, outside the city of Ghent, Belgium. Her parents, René and Martha, came to France after they married, hoping to become farmers like their parents. After two years of hard migrant labor, they returned to Belgium with their newborn baby, Clarisse. They would make many trips back and forth from Belgium to France, during which time they added another daughter, Godelieve, and a son named Jan to the family.

In 1936, the family loaded a wagon with their belongings and returned again to France. This time Godelieve's father found work as a foreman on a large farm near Fresnières in the Picardy region. His wife cooked meals for the workmen. Their oldest daughter had remained in Belgium this time to work as a governess. Godelieve and her brother learned French quickly and excelled in their schoolwork at the little village school, even though they were treated like outsiders.

Friendless, they played in the same woods where the battles of the First World War had been fought twenty years earlier, never imagining the plans of Adolf Hitler would change their peaceful existence forever.

On September 3, 1939, France and England declared war on Germany in response to Hitler's invasion of Poland. Godelieve was twelve. She and her family worried Hitler would invade Belgium; Clarisse was there.

Like many children of farm workers, Godelieve was forced to quit school to milk the cows and feed and care for the chickens and pigs on the farm where her father worked and the family lived. A hard winter gave way to spring, and still the Nazis did not invade. People began to hope they wouldn't, and called this time between September 1939 and April 1940 the Phony War. In April of 1940, that changed dramatically as Hitler began his aggressive attacks on Norway and Denmark.

One day a farm worker came running across the field toward Godelieve and her father, shouting, "The Boches have attacked Belgium and Holland!" The family listened to the news on the radio, wiping away tears for their homeland when the report concluded with the Brabançonn, the Belgian national anthem.

When Holland surrendered on May 14, the Germans were expected to arrive in northern France in fifteen days. French soldiers who escaped from Belgium returned, creeping along the roads like sleepwalkers, in shock from what they'd seen and experienced. Belgian refugees began to pour into France. On Saturday, May 18, the nearby town of Roye was bombed. The next day Roye was bombed again, leaving death and destruction in the ashes. Godelieve's father rode his bike to Roye to see what he could learn and found his friend the shoemaker dead. The Van Laeres prepared to evacuate.

Each night the northwestern sky glowed red. When the electricity went out, they no longer had any news. French soldiers went door-to-door telling the villagers they were pulling out, and anyone staying behind would have no protection from the invading Germans. Godelieve's father knew it was time to leave, even though they had nowhere to go. Some said that safety would be found on the other side of the Seine, at Meulan-en-Yvelines, if they could reach the bridge before the German Army. Despite the distance of over 150 kilometers with a horse-pulled cart on overcrowded roads, it seemed they had no choice. Staying behind, waiting for the German Army to arrive, was unthinkable.

Godelieve argued when Papa told her they could not take the new foal, only a week old. Her pony would die without his mother. As they pulled the overstuffed cart onto the road, Godelieve covered her ears to block out the mare's miserable cries as her foal ran along the fence, calling to his mother.

The road became a river of terrified humanity running away from the advancing German front. Neighbors and strangers from other villages, in devastated bewilderment, asked each other where they were going. Carts overflowed with pots and pans, chickens, and bags bulging with bread and cheese. Cows and dogs trailed behind, their heavy heads hung close to the road.

Godelieve's mother walked alongside the cart, carrying baby Willy in her arms; there was no room in the cart for passengers. In a wagon bed beside them an old man, bundled in a heavy blanket, sat wedged in against boxes and crates like another piece of cargo. He complained in a sandpaper voice, "Here they come again." Godelieve's mother reached up and patted his bony hand and told him she remembered. She had been fifteen years old when the Germans invaded Belgium in

1914. His old head bobbed up and down before he floated down the road, his sad, ancient eyes still looking back.

When Godelieve was a child, her grandfather told her stories about the German invasion of Belgium. He described the Germans as big, hairy beasts, barbarians who pillaged homes, raped daughters while their fathers were forced to watch, and bayoneted entire families.

The day the family fled Fresnières was hot and humid, more like July than May. At first, Godelieve thought the approaching dark mass was a swarm of crows sweeping in from the east. Then they began firing. Two women in front of their cart screamed and fell to the ground throwing their arms over their heads as the planes swooped by above them. Chaos erupted. Screams mixed with machine gun fire and the dull rhythmic thud of bullets hitting dirt. Bodies dropped to the ground like discarded sacks of flour.

Papa looked around for a place to hide. Finding none, he lifted Godelieve and her brother to the ground where they crawled beneath the cart and lay on their stomachs with Willy sandwiched between them. Each time a bomb fell, the children squeezed their eyes shut and covered their ears. Peering out from underneath the cart, Godelieve saw legs hurrying past. Purple wildflowers growing alongside the road nodded their heads bravely before being eaten by machine gun bullets.

When it ended, an ominous quiet settled over the countryside. One by one, people emerged from their hiding places, dazed with shock. Some cried out or wailed when they discovered the body of a loved one, others gathered their possessions and began to set up makeshift camps, too shocked and disheartened to consider going any farther.

The next day Godelieve's family continued on the road heading south. The days were long, the roads increasingly crowded, and evacuees began to collapse from the heat. They were less than a day to the bridge crossing the Seine when they heard an explosion. The French Army, hoping to slow the German advance, had blown up the bridge.

Godelieve's father decided to rest the horses and try to get the anxious animals to eat a little while he thought about what to do next. Godelieve sat on a pile of stones, tying her boot-laces, when she heard shouts and arguing. A German officer and soldier were trying to get everyone off the road. The officer kept shouting, "Take your places." Terrified, thinking the Germans planned to get everyone together and shoot them, people moved off the road, bunching together in a crowded field.

When the road cleared, Godelieve watched a group of German soldiers walking up the road. In front of them was an African French soldier dressed in gray, followed at gunpoint by two Germans who directed him off the road. The German officer grew impatient and told the prisoner to walk ahead of them across the field. When he had gone twenty yards, the man turned and cried out, "I am French! I am from Morocco. Please! I have done nothing wrong." The German officer fired, and the young man fell backward to the ground. A blossom of red grew on the front of the soldier's gray shirt.

Nobody dared to move. Godelieve, shaking, grasped her mother's hand. The officer headed back toward the crowd and shot his right arm forward. "Heil Hitler!" A few voices muttered weakly, "Heil Hitler." The German officer approached Godelieve's father who stood near the front of the crowd. "Why are you here?" he asked, "You have to go back home."

The road going back looked alien and unfamiliar. They passed the decomposing bodies of soldiers and civilians, covering their faces against the sickening smell of death and human waste. French and German helmets dangled from small wooden crosses planted in freshly tilled earth. A German soldier lay dead on the roadside with his face carved out by a knife. Despite her revulsion, Godelieve could not look away. They passed a dead French soldier who had fallen with his legs on the road. The Germans had rolled over him with their motorcycles until his bones were exposed, flat and shredded.

Cows and sheep wore stupefied expressions, calling out for water and needing to be milked. Godelieve felt as sorry for them as she did for the displaced people on the road around her.

Approaching their house, holding their breath in hopes it still stood, they were greeted by the calls of the little foal, Prince. Godelieve ran the last distance in bare feet to greet him and laid her head on his neck crying into his warmth. Other horses, not so lucky, lay dead or burned beyond recognition. The house had been ransacked and the windows broken. Freshly dug trenches were filled with discarded weapons, ammunition, and bloodied uniforms. Godelieve found a dead solider and, with her father's help, buried him.

Godelieve's palms were wet and sliding away from the handlebars. Today the Germans were not firing at her, at least not yet. She had to find the American before they did. If she could convince Papa and Mama to hide him in their home, the Resistance might give her more work to do. Four years, her entire teenage life, had been spent as a prisoner. She ached for freedom.

Reaching the village, she paused at the old church, Saint Jean de Baptist, where the statue of a World War I soldier in perpetual salute gazed down at her. In the cemetery behind him slumbered the villagers killed in the war he memorialized. An unnatural silence embraced the area surrounding the churchyard. Across the road, a movement caught her eye as someone stepped from a small storage barn used by local farmers to store their straw. Godelieve recognized Madame Thérèse who helped the Resistance with clerical work from her husband's office in Lassigny. Her eyes darted up and down the road before she waved. Godelieve hid her bicycle and followed the woman inside.

Daylight flickered between the wallboards casting fingers of light across the floor. When Godelieve's eyes adjusted, she saw a young man covered in straw tucked into a corner. She thought he might be dead, but opening his eyes and seeing her, he smiled, and his straight white teeth reminded her of the Americans she'd seen in the movies before the war.

Dr. Beyer had been visiting a patient in the village when someone came to ask for his help with the downed airman. The airman suffered from shock, but no broken bones would prevent him from being moved as soon as possible. Penicillin was the best he could do for the young man in such a limited amount of time. Seeing a syringe, the American shook his head and tried to sit up. The doctor ignored him, administering the injection through his pant leg.

Both men looked up at the rolling hum of plane engines. The doctor nodded and said, "Les Boches." *Germans*.

Godelieve knelt beside the airman, whose body shook beneath the straw. His brown eyes had grown enormous and wild. She brushed a curl from his damp forehead. Doc Beyer lifted the man's dog tag and read the name: Dean W. Tate.

Turning to Madame Thérèse, Godelieve asked, "Where will you hide him?" Thérèse shook her head and shrugged. "He can stay with us," Godelieve said, trying to sound certain that her parents would agree. Finding places to hide downed airmen had become more difficult. The Nazis grew less patient with helpers, often killing them and their entire family, sometimes in public.

The American's face had taken on the gray pallor of death. He might not survive, and if the Nazis found him in this condition, they would enjoy helping him die.

SEVEN

TAKEN PRISONER

As Dean languished in the storage barn, two members of his crew, David Helsel and John Bernier, were hiding in a cemetery crouched behind a tombstone. They had survived the crash, but three of their crewmates, including the pilot, had been captured.

The last moments in the B-17 had been chaos. Bernier had been pulled out of the ball turret just before it was shot off the plane. By the time Helsel kicked out the waist door, the bottom of the bomber was grazing treetops. The four gunners gathered in the waist of the plane knew it was too late to jump. Helsel and Bernier, along with the radio operator, George Fotenakes, and the right waist gunner, George Lissandrello, braced themselves for impact. Without the bomb load the pilot dropped, they might survive.

After Tate and Gallagher had bailed out, the nose compartment was completely destroyed by gunfire. The pilot saw the front of the aircraft below the cockpit missing and grabbed his chute to bail out. From the bomb bay, he could see the gunners still in the waist. Unable to leave them there alone, he returned to the cockpit to take the plane down.

The B-17 slammed through trees and into a barn, coming to rest in two pieces. The four gunners jumped and rolled from the plane and the burning wings. Fotenakes stood up holding his hand, dripping blood from the finger he'd lost. Helsel ran around to the back of the plane to see if the tail gunner, Bob Kelly, was there. He wasn't.

The pilot, Doris Beam, was thrown from the shattered cockpit window during the crash landing. When he came to consciousness under an apple tree, he didn't know where he was. With sight in only one eye, he saw his plane, its flaming wings on the ground and the fuselage engulfed in billowing dark smoke. Grabbing a tree for support, he pulled himself up and walked toward the wreckage to look for anyone who might still be inside.

To the gunners, their pilot emerged from the orchard like a dead man walking, or staggering, in this case. His eye hung onto his cheek in a bloody mass and his shredded jacket shoulder exposed mangled flesh. Brushing dirt and twigs from his clothes, Beam appeared surprised to see the four men standing together. He asked about the tail gunner, but no one knew what had happened to him. They assumed he bailed out the back unnoticed.

Ammunition began bursting around them like wayward firecrackers and the men ran toward a clump of dense trees just as three Fws flew over, peppering the ground with bullets. A Frenchman followed them and told them to hide in the woods until nightfall. Bernier spoke French and acted as interpreter.

When an Fw landed nearby, the Americans dropped behind a bank. Beam had seen a barn about a quarter mile away
beside a cemetery. They could hide there. Crawling on their
bellies, the four gunners followed Beam down the hill toward
the barn until they came to a road. Beam ordered the men to
cross one at a time and continue on down the hill to the barn.
He went first; Bernier and Helsel ran across the road one at a
time as Beam watched the road. A young Frenchman came
along on his bicycle and called out, "Comrade!" Beam motioned for the men to continue crossing, as four German
soldiers came running. Beam dove into a bank alongside the
road. As the Germans were asking to see the Frenchman's
papers, one of them spotted Lissandrello and Fotenakes.
Grabbing them, he asked, "How many are there?"

"Two," Lissandrello answered.

As the Germans started to leave with their prisoners, Beam
peeked up over the bank and was spotted. One of the soldiers
grabbed Beam and asked, "How many are with you?" Bernier
and Helsel remained hidden only a few feet away. "Three,"
Beam answered. He would spend the remainder of the war a
prisoner, and he never flew again.

Bernier and Helsel went unnoticed. They waited until it
grew quiet before continuing to crawl down the hill. When
they spotted a man driving a wagon toward the barn, they
ducked into the cemetery. Exposed to the Germans on the
hill, they ran, jumping over raised cement tombs until they
reached the back corner and tucked behind a tombstone underneath a large tree. A pale wall of stone nearly as tall as the
men surrounded the ancient cemetery. They bent down as low
as their knees would allow and pressed against the tombstone,
hoping they were completely hidden.

From their hiding place in the cemetery, Bernier and Helsel
could see six German soldiers guarding their plane on a

nearby hill. They had watched a Frenchman engage the soldiers in conversation while behind their backs scavengers
scurried off whatever they could carry; parts of a broken camera, ammunition, tools, shoes, and clothing, despite the plane
still being on fire.

Bernier had shrapnel embedded below his left elbow. Using bandages from his escape kit, Helsel cleaned and bandaged
the wound. The task completed, he suggested they make a
plan. Consulting his compass, he found it broken. Bernier's
compass worked. When it became dark, they would go to the
barn, spend the night there, and in the morning, follow a road
south to Paris.

Jacques Vervel, who owned a nearby farm, had been told
by one of his brothers there were American airmen hiding
nearby, possibly in the cemetery. He drove his tractor around
the cemetery's perimeter, unable to see over the wall. His
teenaged sisters were dispatched to kneel at their grandfather's tomb. Bernier and Helsel heard their whispered
prayers. When one of the girls looked up, she gasped. Her
sister looked up and saw two men peering out from behind
the headstone. Lowering her head to her folded hands she
whispered in English, "Stay here," between the words of her
prayer. "My brothers will come for you."

Later that night, the brothers Jacques, Jean, and Pierre
Vervel returned and led Helsel and Bernier through fields to
hide in their large farmhouse on Rue de Gounay,
Monchy-Humières.

EIGHT

VISIT FROM A NAZI SOLDIER

Godelieve collected eggs in the chicken coop while she waited for her father to return from talking with Monsieur Corrion, the village Resistance leader. Her father was reluctant to hide the American airman in their home, where a Nazi officer—Godelieve's sister's boyfriend—regularly came to visit. Godelieve reminded her father that the officer always waited outside, believing the family's humble home and Belgian peasantry beneath his higher station. And from outside, he would be standing guard, protecting the American without even knowing. Papa had not been convinced. Food would be another problem. There wasn't enough to feed their family, let alone someone else. Still, he had gone to find out what he could about the American.

As she left the chicken coop, she was surprised by the sight of a German soldier standing at the front door. When she greeted him, he removed his cap and asked if he might purchase three eggs. The soldiers from the airfield often ventured out on their bicycles to look for better food than they were given on base. Not everyone would sell to them, and there wasn't much available. The Germans had already taken everything in what many believed an attempt to starve the French. Godelieve's parents believed it best to be kind to everyone, even the Germans. Their neighbors in the village did not agree and freely speculated about the Van Laere family and their loyalty. Being immigrants from Belgium with a daughter dating a German officer provided further fuel for suspicion.

Godelieve told herself to be calm. They would never send a young soldier alone to look for a downed airman. He smiled at her with translucent blue eyes. Deciding he must be new, her heart went out to him.

The German's eyes fell on her mittens, made from a discarded baby blanket and full of holes. He withdrew a photo from his coat pocket of a fair-haired infant with an open-mouthed smile and his father's eyes.

"It must be difficult to be away from him," she said. The young man nodded and returned the photo to his pocket.

A few years ago, Papa told her about meeting a Nazi officer distraught over the death of his son, a pilot in the Luftwaffe. "They are people just like us with great affection for their children," he told her. *Not monsters, but people like us.* That was the first time Godelieve thought of the German occupiers as people. The idea took some time to settle in. Some were only trying to do their jobs and survive the war. German and French alike all waited for a better life to begin, after the war ended.

His eyes filled with tears.

"Don't worry," she told him, "The war will be over soon."

"Thank you, M'mselle. And give my regards to your sister." Godelieve turned and rolled her eyes. She would not pass along his regards to her self-absorbed sister.

Papa returned home and told her arrangements had been made to bring the American to their house before moving him to Paris. No one else would take him. Everything would have to be arranged carefully, and caution took time. Godelieve did not need to ask what changed his mind.

She recalled the farmer in a nearby village who had hidden an English pilot in his barn for a month. When the Germans noticed the family produced more garbage than usual, they searched the house, found the pilot in the cellar, and took him prisoner. They killed the family and dumped their bullet-ridden bodies outside the church as a warning to others who might help the Allies. A rumor circulated that the story about the garbage was not true, a lie the Germans told, and what really happened was a neighbor had reported the hidden airman to the Germans. Information leading to someone aiding an Allied airman was worth ten thousand francs, a tremendous sum when children cried with hunger. Collaborators were more frightening than the Germans. Anyone could be a collaborator.

Dean opened his eyes. In the first moments of consciousness, peaceful acceptance replaced fear, as if all was well and as it should be. His pale hands rested against golden straw. An angry welt crossed three fingers and he studied it with detached curiosity while curling and straightening his stiff hands. Bending his arms and legs, nothing appeared to be broken. He seemed to be alone. Turning his head, a milky light reached in through the cracks between the wallboards. Still daylight. His mind skipped across scenes like a stone thrown across a river. The cockpit windshield splashed with blood. A stench like raw meat. Beam's eye dislodged from its socket. A German pilot waving.

Recalling he had been shot down, he began to shiver. He remembered nothing after hitting the ground. Someone must have brought him here, maybe the gray-haired man with the cigarette. Had he gone to turn Dean over to the German authorities? His heart began to gallop unevenly. The crew—had they been able to escape? Did they stay with the plane during the crash? Were they burned alive? Shivering intensified to shaking. He needed to get warm somehow, and he needed to relieve himself. Closing his eyes, he slept.

The barn door creaking open woke him. A face with a dangling cigarette stared down at him, and Dean recognized the craggy features and white hair. Dr. Beyer anchored the cigarette between his teeth and whispered, "Mangez." Putting his arm behind Dean's shoulder, the doctor lifted him to sit up and offered him a tin cup filled with water. The sweet liquid cascaded down his dry throat. In a metal container nestled beside brown bread lay an uncooked egg. Dean dipped the bread into it and with reluctance took a bite. Before he could drop the bread, he threw up. Madame Thérèse, having stayed while the doctor went to get food and clothes, came from the shadows and knelt to wipe Dean's face with a soft handkerchief. Her worn coat looked as though it had seen many winters and reminded Dean of his mother. Suddenly he felt hopelessly far from home.

The doctor interrupted his thoughts with a question. "Gun?"

Dean shook his head. He never brought his forty-five on

missions and would claim at debriefing that he'd forgotten it. "Again? For cryin' out loud, Lieutenant Tate, I'm tempted to assign you an extra mission." There were too many rules in the military to remember them all, or so he told himself whenever he chose to disregard one of them. Now he realized a gun would have been a valuable gift in a country disarmed by its occupiers.

After helping Dean shrug off his heavy flight jacket, Dr. Beyer went through its pockets, finding them empty except for his escape kit, which he handed back unopened, then stuffed his pants, wet and smelling of urine, into a canvas bag. Dean worried about the old man. The Nazis, finding him with an Allied airman's clothes, would likely kill him.

Dr. Beyer pointed to Dean's Omega watch. Dean looked at the watch and shook his head. It had been a Christmas gift from Hazel Mary, and it was self-winding. The doctor waited with his hand out held until Dean slipped the timepiece from his wrist.

With the doctor on one side and Madame Thérèse bracing him on the other, he took a few tentative steps toward the door. He stopped and shook his head. Falling onto his hands and knees, he threw up.

A sky the color of ashes veiled the sun's feeble attempt to warm the winter afternoon. Dean blinked at it. Across the street loomed an enormous church from some bygone century and a statue of a soldier stood towering over the cemetery.

The doctor's eyes darted up and down the road as he pulled Dean toward a car and, opening the door, pointed toward the backseat floor. Somewhere a dog barked, and Dean moved quickly into the backseat. Last month a copilot had given a lecture about how to avoid capture by the Nazis if shot down behind enemy lines. After the crash, the man had run for some trees. From his hiding place he watched as several Nazis chased down his pilot. Their dogs got to him first. "Don't let the dogs catch you," the copilot concluded, not bothering to wipe away his tears.

NINE

INTERROGATED

The distinct rumble of bomber engines drew Dean to the door of the woodshed. He scanned the sky waiting for the formation to appear. They crossed overhead, as though pulled through the sky by an invisible thread. The bomber stream, what remained of it, had completed the mission to Frankfurt and was returning to England. One limped behind, wounded and vulnerable to lurking predators.

Long after the bombers disappeared, Dean continued to stare at the sky. Lost somewhere in France, behind enemy lines, no one was coming to find him. After a time it grew quiet. A bird chirped. The wind picked up and he returned to the woodshed and closed the door. He examined his clothes: baggy brown trousers with heavy pleating in front and a loose double-breasted brown jacket over a white shirt that smelled of someone else's body odor and cigarette smoke. Shivering and missing his flight jacket, he blew on his hands and plunged them into his trouser pockets. The light from the window would not last long.

Sitting on the floorboards, unable to find a comfortable position, pain radiated up his spine. He strained to listen for a sound, a snapping twig or footsteps, alerting him to the presence of someone coming. Silence. Dean had been told the local resistance tried to find downed airmen quickly after they were shot down to interrogate them and determine whether or not they were German spies. Sometimes the airmen failed the test and ended up dead. His parents might never know what happened to him. A farmer had watched as he and the doctor crossed a field. Would the farmer keep quiet or would he point the Germans in his direction? He'd been told most French civilians could be counted on to help the Allies. But those who collaborated with the Germans were well rewarded, and the French were hungry and desperate.

Trapped and alone, sleep won out.

Dean awoke from a deep sleep to find a man looking down at him. The smell of smoke exuded from the stranger's clothing as if he'd stepped from a fire, and his deep-set eyes were thrown into sinister relief by the light striking up from the lantern he carried. Dean stood and found sensation had abandoned his legs. Struggling to remember what he'd been told to say—*I surrender? Please don't shoot me?*—he decided on, "I am American."

"Dog tag?" Nothing in Dean's training prepared him to decode accents, so he couldn't determine if the man was

German or French. Was he going to be interrogated to determine whether or not he was a spy, or would he be taken prisoner? Aware that one wrong answer could lead to a bullet to the head, Dean's legs began to shake. While the interrogator inspected his identification, a stabbing pain in Dean's temple kept time with the pounding rhythm in his chest.

The interrogator's heavy eyelids drooped as he tossed the metal discs back. "Rank?"

"First Lieutenant."

"Age?"

"Twenty-three." Dean attempted a confident tone; instead his voice came out high-pitched and unsteady. He slipped both hands into his pockets to adopt a more casual pose, as if he was interrogated all the time and found it tedious, or at the very least like he had nothing to hide.

Appearing not to notice, the interrogator stared at Dean's feet. "Station?"

Dean followed his gaze, wondering what might be wrong down there. "Kimbolton, England. The 379th bomb group."

"Om?"

Dean hesitated and the man made an impatient gesture with his hands as if hurrying a child along. "Where you live." Pulling a gun from his waist, he pointed it at Dean's midsection. "Fast."

"Okay, okay. It's been a rough day. 412 Willamette Street, Newberg, Oregon."

"Newberg? United States? Where is that?" Despite his pronouncing Newberg "no bear," his English seemed to be improving.

"It's a small town about thirty miles from Portland."

The man walked to the doorway and looked outside before closing the door. When he turned back a frown deepened the ridge between his eyebrows. Pointing to Dean's feet he said, "No boots."

Dean had just purchased the new British military boots in December, and they were expensive, the best money could buy, and would be good for walking. "I want to keep them." The Frenchman glared at him with sunken eyes. Dean removed the boots, accepting a pair of dress shoes several sizes too big in return.

"The socks, too."

The interrogator stuffed the boots and socks inside his thin coat, and without further instructions, left, taking the light with him. From the doorway Dean watched him disappear into the trees. Exhaustion and nausea washed over him. He bolted outside and threw up. When the heaving abated, he rolled from his hands and knees onto his side, feeling the cold ground against his cheek and the warm tears spilling down his face.

He whispered, "And death shall have no dominion. Dead men naked they shall be one...when their bones are picked clean and the clean bones gone...though they go mad they shall be sane, though they sink through the sea they shall rise again; though lovers be lost love shall not; and death shall have no dominion." Dylan Thomas usually gave him courage, but he was alone, abandoned somewhere in France, and he had no idea what to do or how he would survive the cold night.

TEN

A BOY NAMED CARL

A man woke Dean from his sleep and led him across the star-lit countryside for over an hour until they arrived at a house obscured by the dark silhouette of trees. Inside, the house smelled of mouth-watering food and its warmth embraced him. A young woman with a mop of curly dark hair came to greet them. In slow, careful English she told him her name was Nelly Vincent and led Dean to the kitchen table where she laid a bowl of hearty soup and a plate of eggs before him.

At first, he just stared at the food. His stomach turned over and he feared he might throw up again. Wanting to seem po-lite, he tried a small spoonful, forcing the soup down. He sipped a cognac Monsieur Vincent set before him and felt its warmth flow down to his stomach.

Nelly Vincent told Dean, in her limited English, her husband had been a pilot with the French Air Force in the First World War. He had flown around the world several times and had met Wilbur Wright and Glenn Martin, the pilot and plane builder who founded the aircraft company known today as Lockheed Martin. With obvious pride, her living room was decorated with various medals her husband had been awarded from England, Russia, and Serbia, including an English Distinguished Flying Cross. Dean thought he might be spending the night with the couple, but Nelly Vincent told him they would take him to another home where another American waited.

Dean's heart sank, but he forced a smile for the kind gesture and warm display of enthusiasm. He hadn't slept in about forty hours, awakened at 4 a.m. after less than an hour's sleep, and he just wanted to go to bed. He didn't feel well enough to walk anywhere. His attempts to argue did no good and so he halfheartedly followed the couple into the night.

An hour later, they came to a little village called Thiescourt, nearly hidden in blackness at the late hour. Nelly led Dean into a dazzling bright kitchen at 63 Rue Mélique, while her husband stood guard outside. A pale teenager sat at a wooden table wearing the startled expression of an actor who had forgotten his lines. The boy stood, reached out a hand, and in a quiet voice said, "Sergeant Carl Mielke. 305th Chelveston. Baltimore, Maryland." He looked to be about twelve years old.

Dean reached across the table to shake hands. "Lieutenant Dean Tate. 379th Kimbolton."

Edmond Robert welcomed Dean with a crushing hug and a toothless grin. In 1915 he and his brother, who were both still teenagers, felt it their duty to join the French Army and become soldiers. Fighting a war would be easier than the relentless farm work, they reasoned. The Germans took Edmond prisoner, beat him and left him outside to freeze for two years. He contracted tuberculosis. He hadn't expected to live this long, and impending death had made him fearless. The local Resistance knew they could count on his help.

Madame Robert, a big woman in a voluminous housedress, carried a bowl to the table and pulled out a chair. Dean sat down and said, "Thank you." She smiled and touched his shoulder. A small girl peeked around the woman's legs to stare at the stranger. There was almost no color on her pale skin. Dean smiled at her and she darted back behind her mother's skirt like a frightened rabbit. When her face emerged again, she smiled. At the stove, an orange cat flicked its tongue into a simmering pot.

Across the table the boy had fallen asleep with his head drooping onto his chest. The couple and the child could be killed if they were discovered, or if anyone found out they had helped him. Dean shivered.

Edmond Robert helped Carl to his feet and led both airmen to a bedroom off the kitchen and main living area where they slipped off their shoes and climbed into the only bed. Dean noticed Carl's boots had also been taken and replaced by street shoes.

A burning pain radiated down Dean's legs, and the hope he experienced earlier in the evening evaporated, replaced by lethargy and self-pity. For the first time his body started to experience the aftereffects of what amounted to jumping off a two-story building and landing back-first on cement.

When Dean turned out the lamp the boy began to sniffle. "You okay, Carl?" When no response came, he said, "Don't worry. We'll get home alright. I've met several guys who got out of France." When the boy remained silent, he continued, "They said the French get a real kick out of tricking the

Germans. Rescuing downed Allies has become their national pastime."

"Okay, sir."

"You don't have to call me sir. My name's Dean. You hungry?"

"I am a little."

Dean took his escape kit from his jacket he'd thrown across a chair. "Take my chocolate bar."

The boy accepted the candy saying, "I ate mine earlier. Don't you want it?"

"I'm not hungry," Dean lied, feeling sorry for the kid, probably shot down on his first mission. Hoping to distract him Dean asked, "What kind of a name is Mielke?"

"It's Dutch. Kids used to call me *Chocolate Milky.*"

Dean didn't want to talk, and he certainly didn't want to play nursemaid. Staring at the ceiling, his back muscles contracted into knots on a mattress of knives, and he felt the weight of his exhaustion and all that had happened. For the first time in his life he had no idea what was going to happen next. He thought about his parents, not knowing what had happened to him, which was for the best, going about their life believing Dean safe. From where he stood now in the dark night of a strange place, home was as far away as a distant planet and just as impossible to reach.

Fourteen hours ago, he'd left the airbase on a mission to Frankfurt. If only he'd stayed in bed. Now it seemed worth any punishment. Last night at about this time he and Mac were heading into Kimbolton, where they spent the evening at a pub, with no idea of what the next day would bring. Now he didn't know how he'd ever get back to England. The Germans would sooner or later catch up with him and he'd be taken to a prison camp in Germany for the duration of the war.

Muted French voices drifted from the next room and he

wondered what the man and his wife were planning to do with their American refugees. The family looked hungry, cut off from food supplies by the Nazis, probably living on watery broth they were kind-hearted enough to share with an emaciated cat. They would be better off turning him and Carl in for reward money.

John Martin received the news about his bombardier being shot down from Colonel Preston. The report said ten Fw 190s attacked the group near Amiens, and two of the station's aircraft were shot down. Dean was listed as missing in action. After telling the crew, he returned to his room, to write his father, Major General Frederick Martin.

Dear Dad,

Today they sent my bombardier off with another crew and he was shot down. He had a grand sense of humor, lots of courage. You met him briefly at Thanksgiving, but you may not recall. He is a baby-faced youngster who doesn't talk much with a mouth that in repose droops decidedly. He is about 5'5", 125 pounds. Fraiily built, he has very long arms. Handles himself well due no doubt to playing a lot of tennis. He has a wonderful laugh, the courage of a lion and the coolness of a Mint Julep. He never rattles, even with his guns jammed and a fighter coming in. He just figures it out and hollers, "Jump." His taste in books is universal and he is a voluminous reader. The boys have come to respect him and have a great deal of affection for him. He, on his part, gets a big kick out of the men but seldom oversteps the imaginary line toward familiarity—good man.

We are hoping that somehow they got back to an isolated point in England. The attack came right at the French coast so it is a remote possibility. I feel sure he got out alive and is probably a POW.

Love, John

ELEVEN

A WORLD WAR I BUNKER

At 4:30 a.m., Edmond Robert shook Dean and Carl until they opened their eyes and looked up at him in confusion. The sharp cold pressed a fist against Dean's back. They followed the bulky Frenchman a short distance up the road to a vacant farmhouse beyond the main cluster of homes in the village. Carl spent several hours here the previous day before being moved to Edmond Robert's. A few broken chairs and crates were scattered around the front room. Robert pointed to a stairway, and left them. Carl followed Dean upstairs to a room at the back of the house. Without speaking, they gathered burlap bags scattered on the floor into a pile, settled on top of them, and went to sleep.

As daylight broke, Dean was able to get a good look at the

young sergeant sleeping beside him. Carl's round face appeared colorless against his black overcoat, and with a red and white-striped scarf wrapped around his neck and large ears sticking out from beneath a leather cap, Dean thought he looked like a Christmas elf.

Carl was born on May 20, 1924, and raised in a rural home outside of Baltimore, Maryland. Drafted a year ago—less than a year after graduating high school, while working as a grocery clerk—he had been shot down on his second mission.

That night, at 11 p.m., Dean woke to boot steps on the stairs. He stood. If they were German, he planned to make his surrender as easy as possible. Two figures appeared in the doorway. One of the men carried a lantern and said, "Comrade." It was Monsieur Robert. The light fell on the other man's face and Dean recognized the top turret gunner from the crew he'd been with when shot down. The two men patted each other heartily on the back as if they were long lost buddies, not two strangers who met only yesterday in the escape hatch compartment before bailing out. M. Robert left and Bill limped into the room and made himself as comfortable as possible on the floor leaning against a wall. In minutes, the three men were asleep.

Daylight filled the room by the time the Americans began to stir. Carl yawned and extended his hand to Bill. "Sergeant Carl Mielke, tail gunner."

"Sergeant Bill Lessig, top turret gunner. Glad to meet you." He had a long neck to match the rest of him, and hollow blue eyes glowed from a dirt-stained face. His clothes, wide-legged trousers, a bulky sweater, and jacket, were the best a local farmer had to offer. He collapsed to the ground, removed his boot, and started to unwrap a bloody makeshift bandage from around his foot.

Bill Lessig was twenty-one years old and from West

Chester, Pennsylvania. He was on his eighth mission and, like Dean, had no experience jumping from a plane. He bailed out of the aircraft after Dean as the navigator and copilot stood ready to follow. He had landed in a field and, after rolling up his chute and tucking it into a ditch alongside the road, began walking west, away from an airfield he saw coming down. As he crossed a field, three Me 109s flew over. He fell to the ground, uncertain if the Germans had seen him. The rest of the day he traveled in a southerly direction keeping in the trees as much as possible. When it got dark, he crawled into a thick clump of bushes, ate his chocolate bar, and slept. He woke at daybreak and started moving again. At about noon, he met a Frenchman with a load of horse manure and asked him the way to Paris. He asked if Bill was American. When he said yes, the man answered, "Good." Then the Frenchman pointed to four o'clock on his watch and then to the woods. Bill waited in the woods until the man returned with food and a bandage for his foot. Two hours later, Edmond Robert arrived with civilian clothes, and led Bill to a barn outside the village. He slept for several hours in the hayloft until Monsieur Robert returned. This time he led Bill to his house and fed him before bringing him to the farmhouse.

Throughout the day, residents of Thiescourt slipped into the farmhouse carrying bundles filled with warm bread, hot soup, fried eggs, and sweet, buttery cognac. Dean, Bill, and Carl began to feel like local celebrities. The visitors, nervous about the danger of being found, only stayed long enough to look into the eyes of their would-be liberators, and whisper "Merci," before scurrying away.

One woman wrote a note on a pad that a man who could speak English would arrive the following morning. Through the notepad, she also shared that Carl's crewmate, Arthur Jones, was being hidden by French civilians in the area. Dean wrote on the pad, *Do you know when we will be leaving or where we are going next?* She didn't seem to understand the question, or didn't know the answer, and instead wrote, *Carl landed on a good house. The woman who lives there is well known in the Resistance.* She pulled a note from her pocket that read, *Have patience,* before stuffing her papers back inside her coat and hurrying off.

In between visits, Carl explained what had happened to him and his crew when they were shot down. His pilot and copilot were both shot, and the copilot, named Green, wounded badly. Two engines were on fire when communication cut out. From the tail, Carl saw the waist door go by and knew everyone must be bailing out. He crawled to the waist and followed one of the waist gunners out of the plane.

The day before, he attended a lecture by a paratrooper on jumping, how to stop swinging, how to drop more rapidly, and how to guide the chute. The information helped him avoid a patch of trees, but he grazed an electric pole before landing on the roof of a chicken coop just across the street from where they were now. A woman in the yard screamed and ran into the house, returning a few moments later with her husband. With the help of several farmers, who rushed to release him from his parachute and get him off the chicken coop, they carried Carl into their house at 2 Rue Mélique and gave him a meal and a civilian jacket and topcoat to put over his work uniform. When asked for identification, he showed his dog tags.

The house Carl landed near belonged to a postwoman named Rosa Delnef, a prominent member of the local Resistance who went by the alias Madame de Gaulle. Carl needed to be moved quickly away from the Delnef house because of her known association with the Resistance. Two men and a woman stood guard in the road as the couple, one on either side of Carl, rushed him across the street to the empty farm-house. Doctor Beyer gave Carl a brief checkup, about which he made the following comments in his escape and evasion report: "The doctor was 5'5", well-dressed, and had a car."

Carl's descent had caused considerable excitement at a nearby school. The teacher, Monsieur Martin, unable to maintain order after the children spotted the paratrooper in the sky, and just as excited as his students, allowed them to climb onto their benches to follow the airman's descent. The children laughed and cheered despite their teacher's shushing. Martin, worried the Nazi police would question his students if they had not already found the airman, told them, "You have not seen anything. Especially, you have seen nothing." As the Nazis spilled into town asking everyone about the whereabouts of the Allied airman, nobody had seen anything. They shook their heads, looked into the eyes of the Nazis and said, "No. No American."

Bill removed his cap to run a hand through his matted hair. He looked at Dean and said, "Even behind enemy lines the officers get better clothes than the enlisted guys."

"How'd you know I'm an officer?"

"Lucky guess."

The following night, Friday, February 11, after a long day waiting, Dean woke to creaking on the stairs and a racing heart. From the doorway a muted voice growled, "Boche, allons-y!" Edmond Robert and his brother, through gesticulated French, conveyed to the Americans that the Nazis were nearby, and they needed to leave at once.

Dean's heart hammered, stumbling and falling in the darkness, trying to keep up with the two Frenchmen. Any minute

Nazi soldiers might appear. Tense muscles began to ache painfully. All he could do was keep his eyes on the dark shapes of the men ahead. After walking over two miles, the full moon illuminated the opening to a cave. Robert said, "Stay," and then he and his brother left.

Dean stepped into the black void, feeling his way until he found a cement wall. There, he crumpled onto the cold, damp ground, wet with puddles. Quiet groans told him Carl and Bill had done the same thing. A foul stench like rodents and animal droppings did nothing to dispel his despair. From somewhere in back came a rustle followed by a flutter of wings. Something flew past his head. Bats, worse than rodents and just as filthy.

Escaping France and going home seemed impossible. Hypothermia was more likely. And most likely, a German prison camp where bone-breaking physical labor and torture combined with watered-down cabbage soup in subhuman living conditions would kill only the luckiest. The life he had planned before being drafted had nothing to do with death and killing. He had survived thirteen missions; twelve more and he'd complete the required twenty-five and go home. Back to his life so brutally interrupted. But escaping from France and surviving twelve more missions seemed too much to hope for. Turning themselves over might be the best plan for survival. Bill was injured and he wasn't sure how much more walking he'd be able to do. Huddled close together, the three slept.

When they woke up, Dean could see by the dim light that what he thought was a cave was an abandoned World War I bunker. They were wet and cold. Hunger gnawed deep in his stomach. Dean shifted his weight to sit up and hot daggers seared through his back, sending waves of pain running through the rest of his body. Leaning against the wall, he folded his knees to his chest. Sharp, hot pain split down his spine. Hopefully, getting to the coast toward an escape to England would be a straightforward procedure. He doubted it. He thought about the girl he met yesterday and hoped she made it home safely.

Dean studied the map from his escape kit. He wondered if they should set out on foot and head south toward Paris where they might find help, or at least that's what he'd been told. Get to Paris. From there you'll be connected with an escape line.

Dean decided to investigate beyond the compartment. The bunker was a warren of corridors and rooms littered with dried leaves, dirt, and crumbled cement. Less than thirty years ago, men had hidden here from the Germans, like he was doing now. Following the passageway toward a faint light, he came to another entrance. From outside he saw the bunker had been built into a hillside. In summer when the trees came into leaf the entrance would be completely hidden.

He picked up a rock and threw it against a tree. He didn't ask to fight this damn war. He never wanted anything to do with it. He sat down on a fallen tree and let the tears fall.

He'd accepted his fate, done his job, told himself it was his responsibility, paid his debt for living in a free country—an imperfect country. He remembered seeing Japanese Americans escorted onto trains bound for relocation centers, a name supposed to sound less like internment camps. Drooping under the weight of suitcases and bundles containing as many of their belongings as they could carry. Although they kept their heads down, he saw the dazed expressions and tears. Faces rigid with hatred and fear looked on, regarding the evacuees as if they were animals. And as he waited for a train that would take him to a strange place where he'd be taught how to fight a war, he thought the entire world had gone mad.

Dean didn't consider himself a leader, but Carl and Bill were counting on him. He hated the fact that he was responsible for two boys, both immature and untrustworthy at best. Over his left eye a painful stab picked up a steady rhythm. He'd rather be alone than with someone he couldn't trust, and the idea that his survival depended on someone else was enough to make him consider heading out on his own.

Would it be possible to leave the bunker and look for help on his own? It might be worth the chance, as long as he could slip away by himself. He could go south toward Paris. Dean shivered with the gathering cold and in the fading light turned back toward the entrance, determined to give the idea more thought. He needed to get back to England as soon as possible, get word to his parents that he was alive. With any luck the invasion would happen soon, the war would be over, and he could go home without ever flying another mission.

He returned to find Bill and Carl sitting in the entrance.

Bill asked, "You got a plan, boss?" Dean knew Bill meant no disrespect, and Dean liked Bill's casual, rank-less attitude. "We had a lecture by a guy who escaped after being shot down in France. He said we could count on help from the local people. He said most ended up in prison camps, but if possible, we should hide and try to make contact with the locals." They had been taught to first evade capture and then seek help from the locals, if necessary. Those directions had seemed straightforward until now.

"How did he get back to England?"

"He got passed from place to place, hidden in homes mostly,

until finally he crossed the Pyrenees into Spain where he was rescued."

"So once you cross the border into Spain, you're safe?"

"It's not easy. There's a mountain route into Spain where they were able to avoid official checkpoints at night. Once they crossed the border, they walked to a railroad station and took a train to Barcelona, to the British consulate. This guy was shot down in October and returned to England in December. I'm not sure they even use the route anymore."

Dean studied the silk map again. "Our course took us over Amiens, I'd say that's about where we got hit, right about here." Bill and Carl came to sit on either side of him. He drew his finger down from Amiens to Paris. "I'd say we're somewhere in this area north of Paris." When the boys remained silent, Dean added, "We'll be interrogated, maybe more than once."

Carl cut in, "Why?"

"To see if we're spies." Bill looked at Carl like he had grown an additional head.

Dean said, "Someone looked me over yesterday and asked me a few questions, looked at my tags. You still have your dog tags?" Both Bill and Carl said they did. He tucked the map into his escape kit. "The local people pay a high price to help Allied evaders. The Germans kill resisters and often their families as well, sometimes the entire village. Their children might be tortured, and their daughters sent to military brothels." Dean remembered an airman who had escaped after parachuting behind enemy lines lecturing that every man returned to England cost the life of one Resistance member.

"How will we know who's with the Resistance and who isn't?" Bill asked.

Dean shook his head, "There's no way to know. I'm not sure they even know other Resistance members. They go by different names to protect themselves, and they're careful. Probably everyone who's helped us so far is what's called a 'helper.' Charles de Gaulle tried to link Resistance movements, but for the most part they've remained isolated cells. They work together, always in anonymity."

TWELVE

THE VAN LAERES

It had been a cold Saturday full of work, but for once Godelieve didn't mind. The American and two other airmen would arrive that night, escorted by the head of the Resistance in Lassigny, Monsieur Corrion. Norbert Corrion's occupation as a notaire allowed him to make fake identification and other necessary documents that would allow Allied evaders to pose as French citizens and move across the country to rescue. He worked with the newly organized French Force of the Interior that hoped to unite the various underground movements. Even though the Van Laeres disagreed with his Communist leanings, they offered help to him in whatever way they could.

Godelieve followed her mother upstairs to prepare the beds

in Jan and Willy's room. The boys would move across the landing to sleep in her room. Her parents would never allow her to sleep on the same floor as the airmen, so she would sleep on the floor in her parents' bedroom downstairs.

Smoothing wrinkles from the coarse sheets, her mother said, "We have a few cans of milk, a few jars of canned fruit and vegetables, and one jar of jam. How am I supposed to feed you all? And three extra mouths?"

Food was a never-ending problem. Queuing up for meat in Lassigny was hopeless. On the best days, the first in line might get a fish head if they were lucky.

"Maybe Jan can go out and look for a rabbit," Godelieve said. They both knew he hadn't seen one in over a year.

"There's always the pigeons," her mother said, tugging at the blanket.

"I would eat a cat or a rat before I eat my birds," Godelieve said. All of the cats had disappeared years ago, soon after the rats. Back then she had been horrified to hear people were eating rats, but that was before she had experienced real hunger. "I will eat less and split my portions. Jan will share, too," Godelieve said. Jan's hunger never abated, but he would suffer without complaint to share his food with American aviators.

Back in her own bedroom, Godelieve splashed water on her face and pulled an old sweater of Jan's over her head and stepped from her skirt into a pair of work pants. She had to fasten her pants with a pin so they did not fall from her shrinking waist. She frowned at the round face and untamed curls in the mirror. Like a child, she thought. She wanted to be old enough to do real Resistance work. So far, her work had been limited to carrying stolen gasoline to M. Corrion for transporting Allied evaders. Papa had made sure she understood that she could be killed for doing it, but she didn't fear death.

Without freedom, there was no life. Gasoline had all but van-ished now, like the cats and rats. When a bomber crashed a few months ago, killing a boy and his horse as they worked in a field, people could not afford to care too much. They came to scavenge the gasoline, stepping around the boy's body and his mother crying beside him.

Her thoughts turned to the airmen. She feared they wouldn't be comfortable without American conveniences like indoor bathrooms. They would have to relieve themselves outside in a ditch behind the house or use a bucket inside, and the thought almost made her wish she hadn't arranged for them to stay, but she comforted herself with the knowledge that few houses in the area had indoor plumbing and even fewer were offering hospitality to the men. She remembered the cold December morning in 1941 when her father found her milking the cows and said, "Today, we have more hope. The States have declared war. The war will end soon with their help."

After dinner, Thérèse Pellieu came rapping on their door. "It's time," she said. "M'sieur Corrion will meet you at the Calvary at Plessis-de-Roye, from there you will go to Le Petit Bocage to meet up with the airmen."

Godelieve shoved her hair up under a cap and bundled into Jan's heavy coat. Her father looked surprised when he saw her waiting for him by the door.

"I'm coming with you," she said. He knew better than to argue.

"I'm coming, too," Jan yelled from halfway down the stairs. He was a tall, lean, teenager, with blond hair like his sister's.

"No," his father told him, "You stay with Mama in case we don't come back."

The two-and-a-half-mile distance to Plessis-de-Roye took them an hour to walk. There they met Messieurs Corrion and Vincent—the pilot Dean met on his first night—under a large cross in a grassy field that was known to the locals as the Calvary. They continued on to Vincent's home to pick up the Americans. When they arrived around 8:30 p.m., Godelieve instantly recognized the American officer she had seen in the barn, but there was no time for introductions. Within minutes they were back outside and on their way.

Four miles lay between the Vincent home and the village Canny-sur-Matz. Godelieve led the pack at a steady pace, forcing the men to run to keep up. Her father followed in the rear. They had little time before the Nazi-imposed curfew at ten. If caught with the Americans, they would all be imprisoned or killed depending on their captor's mood.

A light up ahead on the road sent Godelieve diving into a ditch. The officer followed, landing flat on his stomach beside her with his cheek against the dirt and his face turned toward hers. A voice raised in inebriated song grew stronger as it approached. "Arise, children of the fatherland, our day of glory has arrived..." The singing stopped and Godelieve lifted her eyes upward. A man grinned down on her and yelled, "Bonjour, comrades!" Her father hissed for him to shut up, causing the drunk to stumble backward as though struck. Undaunted, he regained his balance and turned to leave, taking up "La Marseillaise" as if never interrupted.

Canny-sur-Matz slumbered in pale moonlight. Surrounded by farmland, the village church spire rose like a sentinel above lightless brick homes and farm buildings. Two hundred and seventy-eight souls, mostly farmers, called it home. When Godelieve came to the first house in the village, a dog's bark shattered the silence, and another soon joined in. She took off running and hoped the others would follow.

Down a small lane and through their walled courtyard, Godelieve ran until she pushed open the door and entered her home. Her father scrambled in last and bolted the door. The Americans stood in the foyer breathing heavily from the sprint. She smiled at her wards. She was finally a part of the Resistance.

She removed her cap and one of the airmen said, "It's a girl!"

"That's the girl who came to see me in the barn after I was shot down," the officer said. Removing his fedora, he extended his hand to her, "I'm Lieutenant Dean Tate."

Disarmed, she almost laughed. Men didn't shake hands with girls in France, but she took his hand in hers and said, "Godelieve."

One of the other men stepped up beside Dean and also extended his hand. "Sergeant Bill Lessig, West Chester, Pennsylvania."

The third airman—who had expressed his surprise at her being a girl—held his hat in one hand and smoothed down his hair with the other. "Sergeant Carl Mielke, ma'am," he said.

Godelieve's mother, in a checkered pinafore and thick black stockings, scuttled forward to wrap her daughter in her thick arms. "My mama, M'dame Van Laere," Godelieve told them, sweeping a lock of hair from her forehead, "And my papa, M'sieur Van Laere," she nodded to her father still standing near the door. Jan introduced himself last. He'd been excited to meet the Americans, but now found himself lost without a common language to ask them questions, having forgotten what little English he had learned in school. Before the war, Godelieve had learned some English, too, but that was years ago, and she felt shy about trying to communicate with the Americans.

As Godelieve's parents discussed the harrowing journey

home, Dean's expression changed. Godelieve understood his concern at once and said, "Not German. Flemish. We come from Belgium." The Americans smiled and nodded. The family spoke Flemish to each other because Godelieve's mother had not learned to speak French.

Godelieve's mother ushered the airmen up the stairs to their bedroom. When she turned on the light, Willy sat up in bed and Godelieve lifted him into her arms and kissed his pale hair. The Americans said hello to the child who grinned at them before hiding his face in Godelieve's neck. Bill pushed on one of the beds as if testing it, and everyone laughed as the family wished them goodnight and Godelieve carried Willy across the landing.

At five o'clock in the morning, Godelieve came into the airmen's bedroom to remove the bucket for cleaning, leaving behind water, soap, and a razor. Asleep, the men looked younger than they had the night before. They were a long way from home and everything familiar. She knew what it felt like to be in a strange country. Children in France had teased her for speaking a different language and looking different with fair hair and blue eyes.

When Dean, Bill, and Carl came downstairs, they found Godelieve scrubbing the kitchen floor. She gestured toward the table and said, "Bonjour." Once seated, Carl pointed to the stove, reading the word "Baltimore" across its front. Godelieve turned from the eggs she was cracking. Carl pointed to himself and said, "I'm from Baltimore." His enthusiasm caught her off guard—he seemed so serious last night—and she laughed. The United States Army had left the stove behind after the First World War, when Canny-sur-Matz had been reduced to rubble, and the Van Laeres inherited it when they took possession of the house.

Godelieve dipped a cast-iron skillet above the burner to

distribute the eggs. Dressed in her best blue housedress, now obscured under a white apron, she still felt shabby in front of her guests. From time to time she turned to peer at the boys, and, seeing them watching her, grinned. Brushing a lock of hair from her forehead with the tip of her ring finger, she returned to the eggs happier than she'd felt in many years.

A pounding came from the front door.

Godelieve's father drew the curtain aside just enough to peek out. "Les Boches," he whispered and pointed his thumb upstairs. He waited for the Americans to rush to their room before he stepped outside.

There were two Nazi soldiers. One aimed his gun at a pigeon while the other stood against the brick wall separating the courtyard from the road. When a shot erupted, the birds flew to rest on the chicken coop's round-tiled roof. Godelieve stood in the doorway watching. She had been given two pigeons in exchange for eggs and now there were almost twenty.

"Why are you shooting my birds?" her father asked.

"It is forbidden to keep pigeons, and we are hungry," the German standing by the wall said.

A black Mercedes pulled up outside the entrance to the courtyard, little swastika flags fluttering on its front fender. A Nazi officer emerged from the car and saluted the departing soldiers with his palm forward, followed by Clarisse, wrapped in a white fur coat.

Amid the unrest during the summer of 1940 after the Nazi invasion of France, Godelieve's father set off to bring Clarisse home from Belgium. The Germans were plundering France, and her family had received no word from her. Her father believed she would be safer at home under his protection. The journey took eight days by bicycle. He found Clarisse living at his sister Louise's house and convinced her to return with him to France.

That summer the Nazis began building an airfield outside the village of Amy, first using young German boys and then French prisoners and local farmers' horses and wagons to carry rocks for the buildings. The farmers could not work without their horses and complained that the Germans had taken away their best workers. Clarisse admired the Germans, impressed by their charm and gifts. Godelieve hated them. In August, young German soldiers arrived to cut trees. They were given free rein to abuse the local girls. Godelieve lived on high alert, ready to defend herself at any moment.

Clarisse bought bread in Amy and the Germans soon learned that she was able to speak English, Flemish, German, and French. When they offered her work as an interpreter, Godelieve's parents refused to allow their daughter to work for the occupiers, fearing that collaborating with the Germans would put them in even greater danger. Clarisse argued that she would be able to facilitate better relations between the French and the Germans and make life easier for everyone, especially her family. A few days after beginning her new job, Clarisse came home dressed like a princess. She asked Godelieve to go with her to Amy with the promise of expensive gifts and clothes.

"I prefer cows to Germans," Godelieve said.

Clarisse passed on information from the Germans to the Van Laeres, who turned it over to the Resistance through M. Corrion. Through her collaboration, she was able to protect her family, and they in turn forgave her, but their French neighbors never did.

★   ★   ★

As Godelieve's father watched the Nazi soldiers leave, he said to his daughter, "Go inside, I will take care of the pigeons." She knew her father would do what was necessary to make sure the Nazis never found the airmen.

Her sister wasn't in the kitchen.

"Where is she?" Godelieve asked her mother, who was preparing to leave. Her mother pointed upstairs.

"Why did you tell her?" Godelieve said.

"She has information for them, and maybe she can help."

Godelieve went to the window to keep watch. Her father stood in the courtyard with his gun idly by his side.

"She just wants to meet them," Godelieve said.

"Your sister would never be disloyal to her family," her mother said. "She won't tell him about the Americans. If he finds out some other way, he will protect us." He had helped them before when Godelieve was caught giving food to a Russian prisoner. Even though the sentry had warned her, she continued to pass bread to the prisoner whenever she rode past the prison buildings on her bicycle. She was arrested and put in a cell to await deportation. Clarisse's German officer bailed her out.

"I think he doesn't come inside out of respect for Willy," her mother said. "After all, he is not the child's father. Go out and gather eggs and talk to him if he comes into the courtyard."

Jan stopped eating when his father walked into the kitchen.

"Take Willy and Mama and go out the back. Stay away until she's gone," his father said.

Dean recognized the footsteps on the stairs as women's high heels—not boots. When a knock came at the door, he opened it. The woman who had arrived in the Mercedes entered the room, bringing with her an intoxicating floral fragrance. She embraced Dean and Bill, telling them her name was Clarisse and her parents were their hosts. "I cannot stay long. I only want to wish you the best of luck." Her blonde hair was cut in a stylish bob and her nails and lipstick a vivid red. Other than the color of her hair, she didn't resemble the Van Laere family. She was a misfit like himself.

When Carl crawled out from his hiding place beneath the bed, his knife in hand, she laughed and said, "How resourceful you are!" He blushed profusely and laid the knife on the dresser. Dean rubbed his chin and remembered he hadn't shaved or bathed in almost a week.

Clarisse told them that the Germans had recently captured nine men shot down the same day as Dean, Bill, and Carl, and possibly from their crews. Despite the German waiting for her outside, Dean wanted to trust her, but why had she come? Was she a spy? It seemed naïve to believe Clarisse a curious girl who just wanted to meet some Americans. He listened and only spoke when asked a question.

She lit a cigarette and remained standing. Bill asked about the soldiers outside. Regarding him through a veil of smoke, she told them the French were not allowed to keep pigeons, and they had come to tell her father to kill them, after first taking some for themselves.

She crossed the room to look out the window, and Dean wanted to ask about the German officer waiting outside. As if reading his mind, she said, "My mother says, 'The closer you are to the enemy, the safer you are.'" Dean understood that she played for both sides and her family knew.

She spoke about her little brother, Jan, working at the airfield Bill had landed near, cleaning the officers' rooms and washing their clothes. When he was eleven, he went to the airfield every day to watch the Germans force French farmers to widen the airstrips. Sometimes they allowed him to help carry rocks. Eventually he earned a job cleaning the officers' rooms and doing their laundry, which he brought home. Her mother was happy because Jan brought good soap for her to use. "Our neighbors think the Germans should not be helped, even if they are paying Jan, but our brother is a real little Frenchman playing both sides," Clarisse told them. "My parents fear he will be requisitioned to work in Germany when he turns fifteen next year. Maybe working for the Germans will help keep him from being sent away. Boys used to hide in their neighbors' barns when they were called up, but that doesn't work anymore."

She sat down on one of the beds as if intending to stay a while. Dean thought she seemed lonely and eager to talk, but he hoped she would leave before the German officer came looking for her.

Lighting another cigarette, she told them about how she learned English by working as a nanny for a family in Belgium, and how her fluency led to a job as an interpreter for the Germans. When she said, "Tell me about your homes and families in the States," Bill stood up as if he had somewhere to go. But she stayed, prodding them with questions until her cigarettes were gone and sweat had drenched the men's shirts.

Before leaving she pressed a kiss on each of their cheeks and whispered, "Good luck." Through the curtain Dean watched Clarisse fold her long legs into the car before the Nazi officer shut the door behind her.

Late in the evening, Godelieve and her father took the three Americans for a walk through the field behind their house.

Having been cooped up all day, the men were restless and needed exercise. The night was dry and cold. After walking in silence, Dean said, "Sir, do you know when we might be leaving?" Her father stopped abruptly as if startled and looked at the young lieutenant. Godelieve explained to her father that the men wanted to know about being rescued and getting back to England.

Her father shook his head and shrugged. "Non."

Dean dug his hands into his pant pockets and silently trudged onward.

"They want information, Papa. They don't know what's going to happen to them next."

"I don't have anything to tell them. When it's time to move them, we will be told, until then, they must be patient."

When the bedroom began to lighten, Dean woke to a pounding headache and hunger. Today was Monday, their sixth day in France, and they hadn't been told when someone would come to take them away, or even if someone was coming at all. Carl snored, and Dean frowned at him. Godelieve had already been in to clean out the bucket they used as a chamber pot, he noticed with embarrassment. None of them wanted to use it, to spare Godelieve, but their fear of leaving the house alone at night bothered them more. He dressed quietly, and left Carl and Bill sleeping.

Downstairs Godelieve sat at the kitchen table with her hair falling over an open book. The floors had been scrubbed and the air smelled of soap. She smiled at him. "What are you reading?" he asked, painfully aware he had been wearing the same limp suit, wrinkled white shirt, and oversized clown shoes for almost five days.

She showed him the cover, keeping her hand inside the book to mark her place, but he couldn't read the title. He noticed the patches on the elbows of her navy-blue sweater as she rose to put the water on for coffee. He remembered reading *The Grapes of Wrath* on Christmas Day sitting close to a warm fire in the dayroom with a gin and orange juice on the table beside him. An unthinkable indulgence from where he stood now. The Van Laeres reminded him of the Joads: tough and fiercely independent, qualities he admired. He believed the Van Laeres to be migrant farmers, like the Joads. They were from Belgium, and worked land they did not own, that much he had picked up even with the language barrier.

His ignorance and naiveté shamed him. If Hitler won the war, France would cease to exist. What would become of the Van Laeres? Hitler would never let French culture and language survive, let alone free the French citizens. Hitler's plan for a master race had sounded exaggerated, but here in France, it was clear that he might succeed. Dean believed his life had been difficult, unlucky even. Godelieve had lived the past four years suffering under German occupation without any of the freedoms he took for granted. He felt ashamed that he would have stayed home and let someone else fight for her liberty.

"I have four thousand francs in my escape kit. Please take it. Your father refused, but I want you to have something in return for your help, and I don't think we'll need it."

"No." She pushed away the escape kit before he could open it. The money would provide food, he knew they were hungry. But in her eyes he saw hope. She believed he could help her in more important ways than money, and this encouraged him. Rescue couldn't be far away. Maybe they'd be back in England in a few days. And for a moment he forgot about being trapped in an occupied country with no plan for escape.

THIRTEEN

VALENTINE'S DAY

On Monday evening, Father François Le Pévédic joined the Van
Laeres for dinner. Dean watched Godelieve smile at the sight of
him entering the kitchen and surmised from the playful banter
that ensued that she had known this man a long time. A handsome man, with black hair parted low on one side, and a boyish
face, he wore a black jacket under which gleamed the white col-
lar of his office. He shook Dean's hand and said, "I always tease
her about her pet fox." Dean followed the priest's gaze to a shelf
where a stuffed fox glared at him with tiny black eyes. "Her father found him alone in the woods. She named him Reynard
after the storybook fox that was clever and brave even though he
was small. He was her first friend when her family arrived in
France and so when he died, her father stuffed him for her."

Godelieve sat down at the table across from Dean, and the priest produced a pack of cigarettes from his coat pocket. Dean shook his head, but Carl and Bill accepted. Father François, as he asked to be called, had known the Van Laeres since Godelieve was eleven years old when he first arrived in Fresnières, the nearby village where she and her family had lived before coming to Canny-sur-Matz. He'd been a frequent visitor to the Van Laere home ever since, and checked in regularly to share news of his Resistance activities. When Allied planes were shot down, he went in search of surviving airmen, making sure they were safely hidden while plans were made to move them to rescue.

As Madame Van Laere served soup, Father François said, "I have news of your crewmates." The priest had found David Helsel and John Bernier at the Vervel farm the day after they were shot down. After he received news of the downed B-17, it didn't take long to find the Americans being hidden with the wealthy farmer known to support the Resistance. He gave the oldest of the Vervel brothers, Jacques, a key to the chapel at La Fayette's chateau near Francières with instructions to take the two men there and lock them inside.

"I asked them where I might find others from their plane. I heard Godelieve had seen one and gone off on her bicycle to find him. I have been busy making arrangements for two men named Helsel and Bernier and now they are hidden on a large farm near my village where they can stay put for the time being." For Godelieve, Father François translated what he told the Americans about Dean's crew and how two had escaped capture and three were taken prisoner after the pilot crash landed the plane.

"On the day you were shot down, an American airman landed on the runway at the Amy airfield. His chute and body were riddled with bullets. The Germans allowed me to see him. I was told that the Germans reported to the American government the death of Lt. Bobb Ross, but one never knows. A German officer took his watch. His family should be told he is buried near Amy."

"He was our copilot," Bill said. "He was right behind me when I jumped, but I didn't see him leave the plane."

A knot twisted in Dean's stomach. If he had hesitated another minute or two, it might have been him shot full of holes. The copilot cared about doing his duty enough to sacrifice his life for it. He deserved to live. Dean, on the other hand, felt unworthy to be alive.

Dean thought about the pilot taking the plane down alone and then being taken prisoner. His eye would need surgery, and he might never fly again. Prison camp—he hated to think about the pilot, or anyone, there. And Beam would be separated from any crewmembers captured with him because enlisted men were kept apart from officers. Rank meant everything to the Germans.

Carl said, "I thought the German pilots have a code to never shoot a man in a parachute."

"Who knows?" Dean said, "Maybe he didn't care much about codes. Maybe Ross was caught in crossfire." Dean remembered the German pilot who had spared his life and wondered again why he hadn't fired—he had waved.

Bill added, "He was a good-looking kid, always a smile and something funny to say, smart, and lighthearted."

The priest rested a hand on Bill's shoulder. "We thought he might have been from another plane that crashed nearby with a pilot named Herbert Rossberg. When asked if he was Jewish, he said he was. He was executed immediately. A brave man."

For a moment no one spoke. A tear trickled down Godelieve's cheek.

After dinner, Godelieve and her mother washed dishes while Father François continued talking and drinking cognac with the Americans. Dean wanted to know what would happen next, and the priest explained that it might be difficult to move them for some time. "The Germans have become more dangerous. They fear they are losing," he said.

He took a drink from his glass before continuing. "A week ago, a number of Jewish children under the age of fifteen were killed at a deportation camp in Compiègne. They were gassed." Dean hoped Godelieve could not understand what the priest said, and that she would never learn the truth that he was powerless to help her.

The priest dabbed his eyes with a handkerchief and said, "Reliable sources tell us they have been rounding up Jews in Paris for some time and loading them onto trains for Germany. On the way they stop at Compiègne to unload what they call 'excess cargo,' anyone they consider unnecessary, meaning those too sick to survive long, as well as children and babies. They execute some. The rest are left to die from starvation and despair."

The priest continued through the side of his mouth while lighting his cigarette, "And not only Jews, all enemies of the Third Reich. Resistance members, communist militants, royalists, Jehovah's Witnesses, Romas, homosexuals, Freemasons, nobles, priests. In the beginning these camps were intended to round up resisters and foreign Jews in order to guarantee safety for the German soldiers." He exhaled a wraith of smoke as Madame Van Laere refilled his cognac. "We knew about the labor camps in Germany of course, but now we understand the Nazis' activities are more sinister than we once believed."

Dean had thought the Allies could do more to help the Jewish people, like bombing railroad tracks going to and from the camps instead of bombing military targets. Now he knew he was right. But his superiors believed military victory the best way to save the most lives. Frowning into his glass, he found his interest in the drink had vanished.

After a moment of smoking in silence, Father François said, "The Germans are preparing for an Allied invasion along the French coast. They plan to evacuate all civilians from Pas de Calais and flood the area to establish a defense line." He explained that the Pas de Calais was an area along the northeastern coast where the Germans believed the Allied invasion would occur.

"They're wrong," Dean said. "The Allies want the Germans to think they'll invade there to throw them off. I'm sure it won't be anywhere near there." Rumors about an impending invasion had wafted through the officers' club; everyone knew something big was coming. Martin confirmed a possible date—sometime in March. Back in Kimbolton, Dean had worried about fighting in the invasion, never imagining he might experience it from behind enemy lines.

They talked about the priest's work at his parish in Francières and how it served as a useful cover for his work with the Resistance, allowing him to round up downed Allied airmen while working as a liaison, carrying messages to small Resistance cells.

"We've been missing in action a week," Dean told him. "We'd like to get back before our families get word of what's happened."

"I promise you, you will see England again," Father François said, snuffing out his cigarette. "As soon as it's safe, someone will take you to Paris and from there you'll either go south to Spain or west to the Brittany coast." As the priest stood to leave, he said, "*Coeur* means heart in French, and you must have heart to trust the people who will save you."

Godelieve served dessert as her father stood up and, with a rare smile on his weathered face, lifted his glass to everyone seated around the table. "Bonne Saint Valentin!" Because it was Valentine's Day, they had cottage cheese with a drop of strawberry jam on top.

The Americans repeated the words, "Bonne Saint Valentin!" and laughed at their poor attempts to imitate French inflections.

When the meal was over, M. Van Laere brought out a radio from its hiding place under the stairs and put it on the table. Although radios were one of the first things the Germans took, many people had hidden theirs in defiance. Soon music filled the kitchen. "Cole Porter!" Bill said. He took Godelieve's arm and circled her around the table, singing, "You do something to me...." As Bill came around the table, Carl stepped forward and put his arms out to Godelieve. She smiled and gave him her hands. They were almost the same height, both blond and round-faced. Dean feared Carl would be heartbroken when it came time to leave.

The back door opened and a man entered the kitchen. Godelieve introduced him as Monsieur Corrion. After introductions and hand shaking, Godelieve explained that he wanted to inspect the airmen's photos. Dean, Bill, and Carl went upstairs and returned to the kitchen with the photos from their escape kits. M. Corrion studied them carefully under the light before proclaiming, "No good." He pulled a photograph from his coat pocket and placed it on the table. The size of his photo was slightly different than those of the airmen, showing less of the men's shoulders and torso. The difference was hardly noticeable, but an important detail easily detected by the Nazis. The Germans continued to change the identification photo format so the Allies would be unable to keep up. They would need new photos.

M. Corrion returned in less than thirty minutes with another man carrying a camera in a black leather box. He
brought work clothes for the Americans to wear. Bill's cordu-
roy pants were tight and too short, and the sleeves of a striped
roll-necked sweater barely covered his forearms. When Carl
emerged from the bedroom wearing a black crewneck sweater
and baggy black pants, Bill told him he looked like a two-bit
bank robber. Dean, in a stained jacket that might have been
white once over a shapeless, brown turtleneck sweater, struggled with a plaid scarf before Godelieve came over and tied it
around his neck. Then she adjusted Carl's beret until it rested
at a careless angle on his round head.

The man with the camera instructed them in English, "No
smile. Look stupid." Dean understood a Nazi wouldn't talk to
them if they believed them to be simple-minded or unintelligent. He began to doubt his ability to carry off the deception
when standing face to face with a German. The charade
would only delay the inevitable: they were going to be found
out and either taken prisoner or killed, and wondering how it
would happen was its own form of torture.

FOURTEEN

DISCOVERED

Tuesday morning, February 15, Godelieve returned home after queuing for butter and found her mother crying at the kitchen table. Godelieve had never seen her mother, usually a passive person who took life's injustices in stride, in such a state. Seeing her daughter, she wiped her eyes and said, "The police came. It was Bosquet and Vasseur. I don't know what they will do."

"They saw the Americans?"

Her mother nodded. Before leaving, Godelieve had reminded the Americans to not answer the door since her mother and Willy were gone, and they would be alone. Godelieve wasted no time with further questions. Her family was in imminent danger, and it was her fault.

Riding her bike, Godelieve caught up to Bosquet and Vasseur not far outside the village walking on the road to Compiègne. They were easy to spot even from a distance, small as schoolboys and dressed in the navy-blue caped overcoats and flat-topped caps of the French police. Her sister had been in love with Bosquet for a while when she first came to France, and Godelieve didn't know if that history would be to her advantage or not. Some French police were known to collaborate with the Nazis, while others did what they could to deflect the occupiers' brutality. Like everyone else, they were trying to survive. Even though the Wehrmacht had given them better pay and new uniforms after training them to detect suspicious behavior, they were still considered potential spies, not trusted, and never allowed to carry guns.

They greeted her in echoed bonjours as she stopped her bike.

"What did you see?" Godelieve said.

"We were told you have animals stuffed by a taxidermist. We only came to tell you it is not allowed," Bosquet said.

Who would have turned them in for such a ridiculous offense? Not Clarisse, especially when the taxidermist had been her father. Her German lieutenant, jealous of the time Clarisse spent with her family, might have sent them to cause trouble for the family, or maybe he suspected they were hiding Americans. But in the past, he had deflected danger from his girlfriend's family. Had something changed? Because the Van Laeres were Belgian citizens, the French police sometimes harassed them by asking to see their papers or other similar invasions to remind them who was in control and that they had no rights in France.

"When no one came to the door, we went around the back and into the kitchen. They were playing cards. We asked for their identification, and then we returned the dog tags to them and left," said Brigadier Vasseur, who stood barely taller than Godelieve.

She studied his eyes, trying to determine if he was telling the truth. They both sounded in awe at their discovery, and she could picture them caught unawares and bumbling through the scene. "What will you do?"

"We saw nothing," Bosquet said and turned to his partner. "Did you see anything?"

"No," replied Vasseur, shaking his head like a child denying any part in a misdeed.

"Do you promise to keep silent?" she asked.

"We do. We swear you can trust us."

Unsure if she should trust them, Godelieve rode away knowing that whether or not they spoke the truth, her Americans would be leaving soon.

During dinner, the Van Laeres conversed in Flemish while the Americans ate silently. Dean had apologized and expressed his fear for the family's safety, telling Godelieve's father they would leave immediately even if it meant heading out on their own. M. Van Laere convinced the men to wait and be patient. Hasty action might place the airmen and the family in even greater danger.

Willy watched Dean scattering torn pieces of bread over his cottage cheese and repeated the procedure in his own bowl. After a few bites he came to stand beside Dean, who lifted the child onto his lap. "Box!" Willy demanded with a rare and disarming smile. Godelieve told the child to leave the men alone and let them finish eating, but she was charmed by the way Dean shook his head at her as if he had understood her Flemish reprimand.

Setting the child on the ground, Dean stood and bent his knees until their faces were at the same level and brought his fists beneath his chin. Willy mimicked the gesture with his small fists clamped tight. Dean pulled up his bottom lip. Willy did the same. As Willy began to jab his fists forward, Dean shifted from side to side, ducking to avoid being hit until Willy's small fist made contact with Dean's chest and the defeated boxer fell to the floor and everyone applauded. Godelieve felt sympathy for the child who would soon have to say goodbye to his "American cousins," as he called them, and knew she would share his grief. The men had become like family to all of them.

During the fight, Monsieur Corrion slipped into the kitchen. Godelieve grew cold as she listened to what he came to tell them. Plans had been made to take the men to Paris. They would leave tonight. He laid the newly made fake identity cards on the table. Dean's name was Louis Robert Roger Kervizic. Godelieve repeated the name over and over so he would recognize it, but he was unable to pronounce it correctly. "Don't speak ever," she told him. The birthdate, June 20, 1918, made him twenty-five. This seemed like another problem as he looked younger than his actual age of twenty-three.

Godelieve made a pantomime of digging and cutting plants while pointing to the word "jardinier" written next to "profession." His new identity made him a gardener living in Caouënnec, Côtes du Nord, Brittany.

"Your hands are too clean to be a gardener," Bill said.

Godelieve remained serious and demonstrated how to hold the identification for inspection and instructed them, "Do not let your hands shake."

"Easier said than done," Dean told her.

Within the hour, a truck pulled up to the courtyard gate. After hasty handshakes and hugs, the American evaders hurried from the house. Dean, the last to leave, turned back and said, "Thank you." The Van Laere family huddled in the doorway with tears in their eyes. Godelieve simply nodded.

*   *   *

While the family ate supper in silence, M. Corrion came to report on the evaders. They were supposed to have caught a seven o'clock train from Noyon to Paris, but the person meeting them in Paris had been arrested and betrayed them. Now, it was uncertain where the airmen were headed, but it would not be Paris.

FIFTEEN

FALSE IDENTITIES

The Noyon train station was crowded with people scurrying in all directions. Dean, Bill, and Carl followed a man who had met their truck in a dark alley. He identified himself only as Maurice. Dean felt exposed. Anyone could see they were Americans, and if they were asked a simple question their escape from France would be over. He tucked his chin down and scowled. He had never liked acting.

No one seemed to notice them, or if they did, they had their own reasons to keep the airmen's secret. People moved slowly and quietly, somber under the weight of the Nazi soldiers' watchful eyes. There were none of the smiles or joyful greetings that Dean associated with train stations. These people would not know joy again until they were liberated.

Under a black sky, the train stood ready to depart, its silver-black body bellowing smoke. Steam swirled around the people waiting in line on the platform. When it was his turn, Maurice presented his identification to the two French police officers standing ready. Dean fumbled in the inside pocket of his jacket for his ID, trying to ignore the sweat running down his forehead and into his eyes. Each officer studied Dean's card, neither looked at his face.

Inside, the air was thick with the scent of unwashed bodies. The airmen followed the guide into an open third-class carriage with benches. Dean let his chin fall to his chest, pretending to sleep, but his heart beat loudly in his ears and his eyes refused to stay closed.

Upon meeting them in the alley, the guide, Maurice, had instructed them to pretend they were sleeping to avoid any conversation on the train. His heavily accented English had been difficult to understand. "Speak to no one under any circumstances. Do not accept a cigarette, someone may ask for a light, and matches are scarce in France. When I leave the train, you will follow me thirty yards behind. We do not know each other."

When Dean looked up, Maurice glared across the compartment at him. He appeared to be young, barely an adult, and he looked hungry. He had not been happy to see them, as other people who'd helped them had been, and something about his tight facial expression and emotionless stare caused Dean to worry. Could they trust him? Who was he? They knew nothing about him other than he looked desperate. Pressed up against the guide on a bench, Carl sat with wide eyes, his face wet with sweat. A woman stared at him unblinking. She had to know they were fugitives. At the Van Laeres', M. Corrion had told them if necessary, jump out the window, crawl under the train across the tracks and run. Someone will help you, he promised.

Glancing at his ticket, all hope faded. Unable to read the words, he searched for "Paris," and did not find it anywhere. A destination must be printed on the ticket, but nothing held any meaning for him. He didn't know where they were going, or how long it would take to get back to England, or *if* he would ever get back to England at all. His mouth was as dry as if he'd swallowed dust and his shirt wet from sweating even in the cool carriage. The train lurched forward and he was able to close his eyes.

An hour later, Dean woke to the screeching of wheels as the train groaned to a stop. Outside the window an illuminated sign told him they were arriving in Creil. Weary travelers gathered their belongings. Maurice stood up and Carl trailed him toward the door with Bill following behind. As Dean made his way through the crowded compartment a man brushed against his shoulder and murmured, "Pardon, M'sieur." Dean opened his mouth to reply and then closed it again. Not speaking was going to be harder than he thought.

On the train platform, several Nazi soldiers stood placidly watching the crowd. One of them turned his head in their direction. Dean looked down. He could feel the soldier watching him, seeing through his disguise. When Dean finally turned the corner, his knees buckled. Maurice leaned against the building smoking.

It was a black, starless night, but once Dean became accustomed to the darkness, he could distinguish brick buildings lining the road. Maurice led them to the door of a brick house and knocked. The door opened a few inches and an eye peered out. Maurice spoke in an urgent whisper while the eye regarded him.

Maurice turned to the Americans and said, "It is not possible for you to stay together." He pointed to Dean. "You, lieutenant, stay here. I come back in the morning at seven. Be ready." Having spoken, he turned and walked toward the road with Bill and Carl trailing behind him like lost children.

A single light bulb hung over a square table in the kitchen. Exhaustion made it difficult for Dean to eat the broth the old woman offered him. She poured the remains back into the pot and led him upstairs. A thin, gray cat followed close at her heels. When she opened a door at the top of the landing, Dean turned to thank the woman, but she and the cat were already making their way back down the stairs. Taking a deep breath, he stepped into the darkness.

A light beside the bed illuminated a sparse room with a small bed and table beside it. Heavy drapes had been pulled closed. As he undressed, his new identity card fell to the floor. He opened it and studied the photograph. Skin pulled tightly over a shrunken face and haunted eyes: his mother's brown eyes and his father's forehead, too big for his face. Absentmindedly he ran a hand through his hair. He desperately wanted a shower.

All at once his body became heavy, extinguished. He slipped under the covers and stared into the darkness. He had been missing in action a week. Had his parents received the telegram? If so, he knew his mother would never give up hope that he was alive, but his father might crumble under the weight of his worst fear realized.

Back home, life went on without him. His parents, his brother, Hazel Mary, ate their breakfast and left for work and came home, ate dinner, and listened to the radio programs, laughing. His father delivered the mail on his rural route to St. Paul where he often stopped to accept a cup of tea from the nuns at the abbey. Dean had never thought about mail as a luxury before. His friends back on base could write to their families and girlfriends and the letters would cross an ocean to be delivered to the intended recipients. It seemed a miraculous thing to him now that he was unable to communicate with anyone.

Dean thought about Martin and Mac and wondered if they would survive. Martin's words came to him: "Sometimes, Dean, I wonder what it's all about." Those words had shocked him and made him angry with Martin for fueling his own doubts when he needed reassurance.

Once back in England, he would not be allowed to return to his station at Kimbolton. Protocol dictated he be reassigned and sent somewhere else, most likely the Pacific. According to the Air Corps, his mission was to return to England as soon as possible, but he had no idea how that might happen or what might happen to him next, and he hated not knowing. He wondered if the guide would even return in the morning. His future seemed as pointless as it was uncertain.

SIXTEEN

STRANDED

Maurice returned at seven in the morning with Bill and Carl, as promised. Snow had fallen during the night, giving the landscape a dusting of fine, white powder. The sky wrapped the world in a gray sheet. Dean trailed Maurice with Bill and Carl's footsteps crackling behind.

At the station, the routine began the same as the night before. Certain that yesterday they had evaded capture by some miracle and today they would not be so lucky, Dean took a deep breath as he reached into his coat pocket for his fake identification. His hand shook. There was no way to stop it. A bored-looking French police officer held out a hand, glanced at the card, and waved Dean along.

Once on the train, Maurice snapped open a newspaper, his

rigid expression giving away nothing. In the daylight, he appeared intimidating, even menacing. The sunless morning gave no indication of the direction they were traveling, and Dean realized he had no choice but to take the journey blindly, one step at a time. Fields and an occasional lonely farmhouse, all washed in monochromatic hues, slid past outside. Inside, he railed against his dependence on others. Placing the ticket Maurice had given him on his leg, he closed his eyes.

Last night he considered giving up. Now, rested, he knew self-pity was useless and could make him careless. If he remained calm and did what he was told to do, he would get back to England. He imagined himself arriving in Newberg, stepping off the bus to be greeted by his parents, his brother, and Hazel Mary, and inhaling the sweet, rain-drenched Oregon air.

At ten o'clock, the train crawled into a large station. Passengers from other trains streamed onto broad platforms. The Beauvais station, with its picturesque architecture, reminded Dean of Timberline Lodge on Mt. Hood in Oregon. Dean and his crew had flown two missions to this area in northern France a month ago. He remembered seeing Beauvais from the air, a sizable town, halfway between Paris and the Channel. For the first time since being shot down, he knew where he was; the knowledge invigorated him like a strong cup of coffee.

The other passengers shuffled away from the station in a disinterested stride, veils of smoke distorting their faces. Dean watched them, realizing he had more to learn if he hoped to fool the Nazis into thinking he was French. No one smiled. He envied Bill, whose relaxed face wore an easy, contented expression, and Carl looked like a native with his grimace of pained discomfort.

They followed their guide until they turned onto Rue

Clermont and stopped outside a brick building with two narrow windows framing its entrance. A sign outside the door
that might have offered them any clue was in French, and was
not of much help to them. Maurice could be turning them
over to the Nazis for a reward.

Stepping inside, Dean's eyesight took its time adjusting to
the darkness. Blackout drapes covered the windows, and the
room swam in a smoky haze. Cigarette smoke rose from
clumps of men who seemed to collectively decide ignoring the
newcomers was the safest course of action. An aging prosti-
tute approached them until Maurice waved her away and she
glared at them before turning back to the bar.

Maurice led them to a corner table and left, returning in a
few minutes with two wine bottles and glasses smeared with
a greasy film. Dean's stomach growled. He hadn't eaten anything today and not nearly enough last night. After filling the
glasses, Maurice leaned in and whispered, "Your dog tags."
The request was not a surprise. He was only asking payment
for his services. He would sell the tags to Resistance members, who gave them to evaders who had lost theirs. The tags
proved an evading airman was not a spy, a necessary assur-
ance that Resistance members required before agreeing to
lend assistance. If a man without dog tags was captured by
the Nazis, he might be killed immediately.

Dean tore at his pant seam where Godelieve had sewn his
tags until one of the metal disks came loose. Maurice stuffed
the loot into his worn, oversized jacket. Indicating the table
with his eyes, he whispered, "Your francs." So far, everyone
who had helped them had refused payment, saying the men
would need the francs to pay their guides and hosts along the
way. Dean hesitated, not wanting to give away all his money.
He wanted to ask how much, but the guide stared back at him
with hungry eyes.

Dean looked around the room before pulling his escape kit onto his lap. Underneath the table he passed his money to Maurice, hoping rescue was imminent and they wouldn't need the money. Bill and Carl watched the exchange and did the same. Maurice tossed some coins onto the table and walked toward the back door. Dean wanted to believe Maurice was just going outside to relieve himself, but feared their guide, his fee collected, was deserting them.

Time passed, an hour that seemed like three, and Maurice did not return. It was nearly two o'clock. The other customers, engaged in quiet conversations, paid no attention. Dean raised his glass to his mouth. Bill and Carl stared back. Carl's round, colorless face appeared ghostly in the gloom. Rank made him the leader whether he liked it or not, and he didn't. He had to do something. They could leave, get away from town, maybe find a barn to sleep in and plan their next move. But they had no money and couldn't speak French, and an unknown trek across an occupied country with no food, water, or money didn't seem like a good plan.

The crowd thinned until only three old men were left smoking at a table across the room. Dean could hear what sounded like bitter complaints about life in general, but they showed no interest in the Americans. Dean studied the man wiping down the bar and decided he looked somewhat approachable, although not exactly friendly. He remembered Godelieve's advice: People will help you.

Placing the coins Maurice had left on the counter, Dean asked, "Can you help us?"

"Oui," the barman said without looking up and passed two wine bottles over the bar without further instructions.

Dean returned to the table, answering Bill and Carl's questioning eyes with a small nod. He berated himself for speaking English and giving them all away so easily. All they could do was wait, and hope they wouldn't be turned over to the Nazis.

When the wine shop emptied an hour later, the barman led the Americans across the cobblestoned street to an apartment building. Ominous gray clouds darkened the afternoon into early dusk. The snow had melted, and the airmen lifted their faces to the cool, sweet-smelling air.

A pale young man with thin hair parted low on one side, wearing dark pants and a partially unbuttoned white shirt, ushered them inside and led them to an upstairs room. He told them his name was Lucien and asked, "What happened to your *passeur*, your guide?"

Bill, suffering from too much wine, laughed. "How the hell do we know?"

"It happens." Lucien lifted and dropped his shoulders in a gesture Dean was becoming familiar with among the French. "Whether your guide knew it or not, I don't know, but he left you in a good place. Our friend here, Jan," he patted the man from the wine shop, "helps us pass downed Allies along an escape route. Thirteen Americans were brought to his shop yesterday."

Relaxed nearly to unconsciousness, Dean forgave the guide for abandoning them. Maurice, or whatever his name really was, had earned the twelve thousand francs, and he wished him well.

Lucien Revert and his wife Suzanne were members of the Resistance and part of an escape line reorganizing itself after the infiltration and disorganization of the Comte line. Underground activities were planned from their home. Suzanne worked at the post office, enabling her to pass mail and avoid censorship, as well as intercept letters intended to expose Resistance members to the Gestapo. In doing so she saved many lives.

While Lucien and Jan talked, Dean, sitting in a chair by the window, fell asleep. His head falling forward startled him awake. Lucien paced, waving his arms in huge circles for emphasis as if conducting an orchestra. He had a long, earnest face and the determined look of a young revolutionary. When he noticed Dean watching, he told him about the bombing raid yesterday, gesturing toward the window where he had watched the P-51s attack. The British raids at night had been more successful.

Lucien told them the Nazis were using French soldiers to renovate a nearby building into their headquarters. The Nazis forced the African soldiers to go on working out in the open during bombing raids while they hid in shelters. He spat on the floor and ran a hand around his neck. "They have no regard for human life, especially if your skin is not the same color as theirs." Dean had seen a similar kind of hatred for Nazis in the Welsh hostess and wondered if this depth of emotion was what fueled people like Lucien to do the dangerous work they did.

Jan said something quietly and offered Lucien a cigarette. He nodded and accepted it with a shaking hand. After lighting it, he threw the match on the floor and tilted his head back to exhale. "I think they grow tired of war. Last week I watched a soldier drop a propaganda leaflet, the ones airdropped by the British, on the street. An officer who saw him do it picked up the leaflet and knocked the soldier around a little, without his heart in it. They don't like France. They want to go home."

Dean didn't care much about the Nazis at the moment. His head swam in an alcohol-induced haze as he looked longingly at the bed where Carl and Bill sat slumped forward in exhaustion. Sleep was too much to hope for. A young woman entered the crowded bedroom carrying glasses and a bottle. Dean, not wanting to be rude, feared if he drank any more wine he would pass out. He accepted her offer politely and took a small sip. When he smiled up at her, she said, "Calvados, Apple Jack," and extended her hand. "I am Suzanne, Lucien's wife."

Lucien asked if they had any francs. Dean shook his head and told them the guide took all their money. Lucien's forehead wrinkled in consternation, and Dean, sensing the problem, knew a meal wasn't coming any time soon.

Downstairs in the kitchen, Suzanne apologized while serving a broth resembling old bath water. Dean, having eaten nothing all day, forced the soup down, unsure when he'd eat again. Bill, he noticed, had somehow managed to finish his soup before anyone else and asked the couple about their work.

Suzanne explained that they weren't able to get enough food to keep evaders for any length of time. Lucien worked at the airfield near Tille, and although he earned less than a hundred francs a day, he could steal wire, switches, and electrical equipment from the airfield for Resistance work.

Suzanne told the Americans about a family outside of Beauvais caught hiding an American airman. "The Gestapo shot the whole family." The room suddenly turned cold. Dean thought of Godelieve and her parents, and her brother, and Willy. He imagined them in the courtyard being shot one at a time, as easily as the German shot the pigeons: Monsieur Van Laere first, and next, Madame Van Laere, crying and begging for her children to be spared—Jan, Willy, and finally Godelieve.

Suzanne had moved onto another topic. "When you return to England, tell them we need more guns. We have a machine gun and small arms and ammunition here, but we need much more. The Sten guns dropped by the British were taken by people in the country and never reached us here in town."

Bill shook his head at the impossible request. "I imagine it's hard to drop machine guns accurately on a town. We have enough trouble with bombs."

The next day around seven p.m., a sharp knock at the front door brought an abrupt end to conversation. Lucien returned to the kitchen with a tall man wearing a three-piece suit and horn-rimmed glasses. His name was Gilbert Thibault and he would drive the airmen to their next destination.

In 1940, Thibault, captured while serving in the French Army, escaped from a German prison camp. In March 1943, he created the Alsace line, an escape route for soldiers, officers, and others wanting to join the Free French forces in Spain. By August 1943, he had concentrated his efforts on the Alsace line in France, passing through Allied airmen and any information that could serve the Allied cause. He told them he was an attorney, which had been his occupation before he was called up for military service in 1933. The Americans had no idea of Thibault's real identity or importance.

There were other American airmen being hidden in the area, and a plan existed to bring them all together. The only obvious problem seemed to be that Gilbert Thibault had been drinking, and more than a substantial amount. He was full-on drunk.

SEVENTEEN

FIVE EVADERS

Gilbert Thibault navigated the dusky winding roads like a madman, sending the three Americans hiding on the backseat floor slamming into one another. Driving carefully would draw attention, as the French never drove with caution. Thibault talked to himself as he drove, sometimes shouting out happily, and for no apparent reason, "Oui!"

They reached the village called Ons-en-Bray as the sky lost the last of its color. Dean stumbled from the car outside a stone cottage, which served both as an inn and a cover for hiding Allied airmen. From the fence hung a shingle identifying the establishment as La Maison Bleue. A tiny white-haired woman trotted toward them, kissing Thibault and patting his cheek, before waving her hand like a tiny sail as he sped away.

She hurried the three Americans upstairs to a room where, once safely deposited, they fell fully clothed on the only bed and slept.

It was ten a.m. when the innkeeper knocked lightly and entered the room carrying coffee and bread. If she was surprised to find the men fully dressed and asleep on top of the bedspreads, she said nothing.

After eating, Dean looked out through a transparent curtain to a square across the street. He wondered about the prudence of hiding Allied evaders in the center of a town when he heard a rhythmic sound like drumbeats growing louder. For a brief moment, he expected a parade to come up the street—then he remembered where he'd heard the sound before and what it meant. Boot steps. Nazi soldiers appeared, with confident faces held in perfect impassivity, guns slung over their shoulders, goose-stepping in a tidy rectangular formation. Dean counted twenty. Despite Lucien Revert's comment about their being tired of the war, they appeared well-fed, strong, and healthy. Bill came to stand beside him and whispered, "Shit."

In the evening, boot steps on the stairs jolted the men awake. Thinking the Germans had found them at last, the men catapulted to their feet. Around the door, a grinning face emerged. "Anyone order room service?" the stranger asked in an American accent, entering the room with his hand extended before any of his stunned comrades could speak. His name was Everett Stump, and the shorter man behind him was Carlyle Van Selus. Another man by the name of George Buckner entered last.

The innkeeper brought up cognac and cigarettes and a celebration commenced. Everett exhaled a stream of smoke and smiled. It seemed a good sign to be among other Americans; they were being gathered together, which gave Dean hope they might soon be on their way back to England.

Everett was tall and lanky with drooping eyes and mouth that gave him a sad, hangdog look, which—along with the beret he wore—made him look French, an enviable fact under the circumstances. Everett's baggy pants were too short and his heavy overcoat two sizes too big, and his smile was guileless. Dean immediately liked him. He came from Huntington, West Virginia, where he had worked as a mechanic, truck driver, and welder before enlisting. Van and Everett were both gunners from the 92nd bomb group stationed in Podington, England, and were on the same plane when shot down during the air battle that downed Dean and the others on February 8. Up until this point, a schoolteacher had hidden Van and Everett in his home in a village called Crèvecœur.

Carlyle, or Van, as everyone called him, looked like a corn-fed farm boy with a large head, full lips, and deep-set eyes. Like everyone who met the size requirement to fit into the claustrophobic ball turret, he was small. A mass of wavy brown hair was combed straight back off his forehead. Under a black trench coat, he wore heavy work pants with suspenders and a thick turtleneck. Raised by his grandparents in Minnesota who offered him the deed to the farm if he stayed home, he enlisted anyway, seeking adventure.

Van suggested they leave and try to get to Spain. Waiting made him feel vulnerable. Dean listened to the men discuss various plans without saying a word. He didn't like Van Selus and the arrogant way he explained his idea about how to escape when he knew as little as the rest of them, but Dean would not let that influence his behavior. He wanted to say, "Go ahead and leave," but Van would be caught and expose the others.

Instead Dean said, "If we leave, we run the risk of never

getting any help. And it's a long way south through France. We'll likely be captured. We just need to be patient. It may take months to get out." As the only officer, the men would look to him for leadership. He wasn't sure what they should or should not do, but he wasn't going to let Van call the shots.

Bill said, "Waiting is hard, but it's better than a German prison camp."

The following day, two men from Stump and Van's crew visited: tail gunner Sergeant Francis Higgins and radio operator Staff Sergeant Robert Sidders. They stayed only an hour before a guide took them away. George Buckner left with them. It had been arranged that Higgins, Sidders, and Buckner would be hidden together, and Dean, Bill, Carl, Van, and Stump would be taken to another hiding place. Smaller groups of men were easier for local farmers to feed and for the Resistance to move across the country.

Sunday night around eight-thirty, a twenty-one-year-old Frenchman named André Duval came to the inn. He was a stocky young man with piercing black eyes in a wide, child-like face. Although he didn't speak English, he conveyed to the men that they would be following him to their next destination. The innkeeper seemed to know him and served coffee spiked with cognac before they ventured out into the cold night.

Once out of the village, André led the five evading airmen across barren, muddy fields the two-mile distance to the Duval farm in a cluster of farms called Villers-Saint-Barthélemy. Walking felt good at first, but they had been kept indoors for two weeks, and their legs quickly tired and ached by the time they reached the farm an hour later. And the moonless dark imitated blindness, causing Dean to stumble and fall more than once.

They left the road and entered a cavernous barn bigger

than any Dean had seen in Oregon. Before they could ask any questions or offer their thanks, André left with the lantern leaving them alone in the darkness.

A dog with the head of a beagle, a lean body, and a tiny stub for a tail dropped with his head on his paws as if he was sorry about the whole situation. Dogs were pacifists, Dean believed.

Van had slept in straw before and suggested they dig a hole and cover themselves with it. After digging out a nest and finding a comfortable position, they pulled straw over their bodies. Still, the men shivered through the long night.

In the morning, André woke them with a hearty bonjour. He carried a basket of fresh bread and fried eggs in a tin container and a pitcher of water. Later in the day he returned with fresh water and a razor. Smiling broadly, he tossed Dean a large cake of soap. Dean tested the water. It was cold, but he was too happy to care. None of them had bathed since leaving England.

André also brought blankets, instructing where to bury them should Germans come. The men could run away across the field and hide in the trees, but exposed blankets would be evidence and the Duval family would pay the price.

The day stretched into eternity. They gathered around Dean's silk map and determined their location was somewhere north of Paris and south of Beauvais. As night fell, it became too dark to see inside the windowless barn. Stomachs growled. They huddled together, pulling straw over their bodies for the small amount of warmth they imagined it offered. Carl snored softly. There was nothing to do but think about food while they sat in the silent darkness shivering and waiting.

It had been dark for hours when André came in carrying a lantern and a machine gun. Grinning, he pointed the gun around the barn, mouthing the sound of spraying bullets like a boy playing war. "Debarquement!" he said, lowering the gun, and his long, sandy-colored hair fell across his face.

The men stared back at him. Everett, who had taken a year of French in high school, said, "The landing. He must mean the invasion."

André nodded and smiled. "Oui. Je suis prêt!"

"Is it happening?" Carl asked, sitting up quickly.

"I think he means to tell us he's ready for it," Everett's words were cut off by the moan of a horn from somewhere outside.

"Allons-y!" André sang out, waving for the men to follow him.

André's mother, Héloise Duval, stood in the front doorway to the old farmhouse holding a small trumpet. She hugged Dean before he crossed over the threshold, and each man who followed received the same. A long, timber-beamed living room ended at an enormous fireplace, and the wood-planked floors were worn smooth by generations of use. Dean followed André through an arched doorway into a dining room where the family, all talking at once, gathered around a spacious table. Partially visible beyond the dining room was a provincial kitchen where gray tufts of dried lavender hung from the ceiling's exposed beams.

Madame Duval, an ample woman, smiled and placed a tureen of potato soup on the table like an offering. The sister, Rolande, studied the Americans from beneath dark lashes. She had André's wide, friendly face, but mahogany-colored hair pooled around her shoulders. The younger brother, Henri, was fair-haired like André and as boisterous as his siblings, but was closer in size to an eight-year-old than a thirteen-year-old. Dean wondered about the toll near-starvation had taken on a generation of French children.

Using gestures and a large French-English dictionary, André apologized for the late hour, saying it was the safest time to bring the Americans inside the house. Maurice Duval, round faced and stocky like his son, kept his head bent to his soup while his wife flitted in and out of the kitchen like a hummingbird, placing her hand on her son's shoulder whenever she passed behind him. Dean watched, reminded of his own mother.

While the Duval family talked in a brisk exchange of unintelligible language, Dean wondered about the danger their presence placed on the family as he studied the Americans, a motley crew, sitting around the table. They were five now, and five evaders would be more difficult to move through public places.

Bill asked about the machine gun, and André found the word "field" in the dictionary and pointed outside to emphasize where the gun had landed. The British had been dropping guns and ammunition, arming the French citizens for the coming invasion. One flaw in the plan was the guns were falling into the hands of farmers with no experience using weapons.

Dean, wiping the last of the creamy soup from his bowl with a piece of bread, smiled at André and said, "Thank you, merci." André, waving away the gratitude, wanted to know if there was anything he could supply for the airmen. Van found the word alcohol in the dictionary. The chafing of his pants had caused him to develop blisters around his stomach and hips, and he thought alcohol might clean and dry them. André provided a bottle of whiskey and told him to take it back to the barn. Later, when Van dabbed the whiskey on his sores sparingly, he said he hoped the family didn't think he had asked for it to drink. Tempted, no one drank any, not wanting to use something probably in short supply.

After Rolande cleared the table, Monsieur Duval lifted a kitchen floorboard and retrieved a radio hidden in the crawl-space, twisting the dial until the BBC came in over the static. They translated the French broadcast for the Americans. Eight hundred Allied bombers from the 8th Air Corps had successfully rained destruction on Berlin. It was being called the most intense air raid to date. Bombings continued in London, killing and injuring civilians and destroying homes and buildings. Meanwhile in Estonia, the battle for Narva raged on between the Soviet Union and Germany. German losses were reported to be high. Hopeful news. The Americans speculated about how much longer Germany would be able to hold out until they ran out of men and boys. Monsieur Duval poured hefty shots of cognac, raising his glass to the 8th Air Corps members sitting around his table. Dean thought about his crew and hoped they had survived the stepped-up effort to reduce Berlin to rubble.

André wanted to know when the invasion would take place. Dean wished he could tell him. There had been rumors it was planned for March—that was less than ten days away, a sobering idea. If they were still in France during the invasion, there would be no escaping the chaos. They needed to get out of France before it happened.

EIGHTEEN

NO END IN SIGHT

The following day, André's friend René Buffard came to meet the Americans. He was a student living with his parents in Beauvais and planning to attend the Cité University in Paris to study dentistry in the fall. His clean, wide-legged trousers were cinched with a wide leather belt, and a white shirt gleamed from beneath a loose suit jacket. René bombarded them with questions about the States, a place that fascinated him and that he dreamed of visiting one day.

René told them how André had used the barn as a hiding place in 1942 when he had been requisitioned for the Service du Travail Obligatoire, the compulsory work service the Nazis used to deport French civilians to forced labor camps in Germany. The Nazis searched the barn and found no trace of him. André disappeared into the night, walking thirty kilometers north to a farm in Feuquières where other people his age, using false names, posed as farm workers to avoid being deported to Germany.

During his two years there he met René and other young rebels, communists mostly, who wanted to free France. By the time André and René returned home they were official members of the French Resistance, passeurs, and given code names—René's was Dual Six and André's P1. Because they had laid dynamite on train tracks, a reward was being offered for information regarding their whereabouts. Forced to hide from Gestapo and French police, and a prisoner in his own home, André brought with him his first responsibilities: to collect, convey, and hide Allied airmen shot down in the region. He had only been home a few months and was trying to keep a low profile. These were his first airmen, a test he needed to pass, and a mistake could mean death to him and his family.

Dean listened with fascination. He admired René's bravery and the calm, matter-of-fact manner in which he told of his exploits, without a trace of arrogance. There was a lack of artifice about him, an unabashed innocence in the questions he asked about Dean's experiences in the war, more interested in the Americans' lives than his own. He was someone Dean would consider a friend under different circumstances that allowed for such extravagances.

Last year, Dean had read in the newspaper about the ambush and shooting of a German officer by the Resistance. When the Germans couldn't determine who was responsible, they took fifty hostages, one a schoolboy under eighteen years of age. They were taken to a quarry and shot by firing squad. The Nazis buried the bodies in nine different cemeteries to avoid shrines to the martyrs. Though it was forbidden to lay wreaths on their graves, the French did so anyway. President Roosevelt issued a statement condemning the killings and warning the Nazis they would be held responsible for the crimes and punished after the war. The Nazis responded with an edict threatening to execute innocent French citizens any time a German was murdered. The Resistance, undeterred, would look for other ways to terrorize the occupiers.

René told them that because their connection in Paris had been caught the evening they left the Van Laeres, they had ended up on a longer, improvised route. Others in the area were hiding Americans. René heard a rumor that someone nearby was harboring Dean's copilot. Dean told René that they had heard the copilot died on a runway near where they were shot down, and René explained that most of the information they received was hearsay and unreliable. The Americans would have to wait until they returned to England to learn the fate of their crews.

Behind the barn in the snow-dotted pasture, Dean blinked at the bright white sky. The countryside and rolling hills in the distance, like the hills around his home in Newberg, made him feel homesick. René, camera in hand, posed the airmen underneath a leafless oak tree. Van stood between Bill and Dean with his arms draped over their shoulders. Beside Bill, Carl bent under Everett's arm.

A cold wind picked up, and the sun vanished into the clouds. Dean and René turned from their conversation to see Bill and Everett racing across the pasture. The little dog named Bing ran beside them, barking and smiling with pleasure. Before long all of them ran across the muddy grass, chasing each other like the boys they had been only a few years ago, and for a time the war and their precarious position were forgotten.

When the light faded, wisps of pink cirrus clouds hung over the horizon. A week ago they were dancing in the kitchen with the Van Laere family. Dean wondered where they would be a week from now, and had no idea.

It rained for days, a cold, sleety mix that penetrated the bones. Although temperatures climbed above freezing during the day, the snow refused to retreat. The Americans grew more bored and listless with each passing day, waiting for the evening meal inside the warm house with the Duval family. When they finished eating, and had politely refused second helpings, Dean stood and thanked Madame and Monsieur Duval, before leading the others back to the barn.

Tonight, after returning to the barn, Dean noticed someone missing. "Where's Bill?"

"I dunno."

"Maybe he was captured between here and the house." Laughter.

"By the mud." More laughter.

Dean went back outside to look for him. He had only taken a few steps into the darkness when voices drifted from behind the barn. He found Bill and André's sister Rolande sitting on discarded crates. Rolande said good night and kissed Bill's cheek before she disappeared around the corner.

Bill apologized, but his voice held no remorse. "The rain stopped, and I thought..." He shrugged expansively like a native. They leaned against the barn and looked up at a canopy of stars.

"Rolande wants me to stay," Bill said. "And I thought I might be able to help them during the invasion."

"That's up to you, I won't stand in your way. You might be a liability. If you're found here, the family might be killed, and who knows how long it will take. It could last months or longer."

Bill remained silent for a moment in the darkness. "I haven't been home in so long. I'm not sure I want to go back. No one will know me anymore, and I'll be different. I can't go back to being who I was before, ya know? I don't want the humdrum job I had. I want something more." Dean raked his fingers through his hair. They had all changed and couldn't go back to who they were before the war. Bill continued, "René said they call us parcels. That's their code for us, for evaders, so they can pass messages saying they have some parcels coming. It's like a movie. Hey, maybe they'll make a movie about us!"

Dean stared into his palms as though they might provide some solace. Ever since landing in France, a single-minded determination to escape and get home had consumed him. Now he wondered, to what? The life he had planned was over and nothing would ever be the same again. While Dean appreciated Bill's ability to embrace the situation, he didn't feel the same. Today was Tuesday, the twenty-second of February, and he had been in France for two weeks. His parents, whether they had received a telegram or not, wouldn't know if he had been taken prisoner, or was injured or dead. He had hoped to save them the grief. If he could somehow get word to his parents, let them know what was happening, all would be bearable.

NINETEEN

NEWBERG

A gray, blustery morning had given way to a deluge of cold rain. Tracie Tate stood in the entryway holding the Western Union telegram. The young man who had delivered it asked if she was alone and offered to stay with her. She shooed him away. Her hands shook as she read.

FEBRUARY 25, 1944

MR. AND MRS. WILLIAM F TATE

REGRET TO ADVISE THAT YOUR SON
LIEUTENANT DEAN W TATE IS REPORTED

MISSING SINCE FEBRUARY EIGHT WHILE
ON MISSION TO GERMANY STOP LETTER
FOLLOWING

THE ADJUNCT GENERAL

Will came home from his morning deliveries and found his
wife on the floor. He knew before he saw the crumpled telegram lying beside her that they'd received news about Dean.
They leaned against each other on the entry rug as Will slowly
picked up the piece of paper and read it.

Will had the rest of his mail to deliver. He helped his wife
to bed and placed a cup of hot tea on the bedside table. Every
day Will drove past the pulp mill on his route and honked a
hello to Hazel Mary Houser who worked there. Today he
decided to stop. Hazel Mary saw him walk in and knew something had happened to Dean. Will's sallow skin sunk low off
his face and he was bent over even more than usual.

"It's Dean," she said. Will nodded. "I can leave right now
and go home with you."

Hazel Mary climbed the stairs to Tracie's bedroom.
Dean's mother lay on the bed staring at the ceiling. Hazel
Mary took her hand and said, "You must continue writing
to him. Think how happy he'll be to receive a big pile of
letters when he returns to England. We'll all write to him,
every day. And we'll go on living as if he is coming home.
Writing will give us hope. He is missing in action, not killed
in action. He'll make it back to England. If anyone can do it,
it's our Dean."

Tracie smiled weakly and nodded, feeling certain that Dean
was a prisoner. She couldn't bear to think of him hurt and

mistreated while comforted by the fact that he wouldn't be flying any more missions.

Later that night when Tracie couldn't sleep, she drifted through the living room and kitchen. Tears blurred her vision as she touched the kitchen table where they had spent so many happy times together, her boys eating pie or some other treat she had made for them, joking and teasing each other.

Her mind conjured scenes of her son alone and cold, crumpled on the dirt floor of a German prison cell. To crush the haunting images, she opened the drawer where she kept her journal and flipped on the light. In a shaky hand, she wrote, "Our precious Dean is missing in action. Oh! God, please care and protect him. Oh, my precious lad, are you hungry or cold? Wayne says Pub is okay."

Turning to the page dated February 8, she read the entry written on the day her son had been shot down.

Tuesday,

Home from work; found a letter from Wayne and card from Reola. Ironed over half my curtains. Will washed windows for me. Bless his heart! Saw Lassie Comes Home. Good picture.

She considered the time difference between Oregon and France, unsure how many hours were between them. It was likely that at the time she had written this entry, Dean had already been shot down. As she slept without so much as a dream about her lad, his life had been in terrible danger. Did he bail out of the plane using a parachute or did he go down with the plane? What horrors had he seen? Was he a prisoner in Germany? What would they feed him? Was he hurt?

Dead? No. She would not think it. Thinking it invited the possibility. She would never accept the gold star. She motioned with her hand, pushing its specter away.

She read on to what she had written the following days, as if looking for a clue that her mother's intuition had suspected distress.

Wednesday, February 9, 1944
Most beautiful night! After getting home from work, I ironed rest of curtains and did some other ironing. Will helped me hang all the curtains and washed the outsides of the windows. Letter from Rachel.

Thursday, February 10, 1944
Worked all day at the factory, had to sort filberts and it makes me sort of nervous. Got home, made 2 batches of candy for Wayne and Dean, fudge and penuche.

Monday, February 14, 1944
Ate up the town to celebrate Valentine's Day. 2 letters from Dean. Wrote to him.

She never suspected, and Dean had not received her letter, nor any of the letters she'd written since. There would be no more letters from him. She would rely on her faith, as she had done her entire life. Dean was alive, and she would accept no other thoughts.

As the endless days wore on, her heart began to beat irregularly and hard, waking her in the night. She began to have fainting spells, sometimes at the store. A visit to the doctor revealed her blood pressure at 190.

★   ★   ★

It was a wet Saturday afternoon. Hazel Mary was consulting her mother's list in the produce section and didn't see Mrs. Allen approaching.

She jumped when she heard, "Good afternoon, Hazel Mary." Mrs. Allen's daughter had married a man who now built planes for Boeing in Seattle. He had declared himself a pacifist and registered as a conscientious objector. As the war years commenced, in Newberg, mothers of boys killed in action looked bitterly at Quaker mothers whose sons were safe at non-combat jobs.

"Has there been any word about Dean Tate?" Mrs. Allen asked.

"No, I'm afraid not. He's only missing, so I'm sure he'll make it back to England."

"Yes, well, it's a shame about Dean having been a bombardier. Dropping bombs and causing the death of innocent people will be on his conscience for the rest of his life."

Hazel Mary could feel the heat rising up her neck. "At least he wasn't building the planes that dropped the bombs," she said much louder than she'd intended and walked briskly out of the store.

February 28, 1944

Dear Mr. Tate,

This letter is to confirm my recent telegram in which you were regretfully informed that your son, Second Lieutenant Dean W. Tate, 0-679,251, Air Corps, has been reported missing in action over Germany since 8 February 1944.

I know that added distress is caused by failure to receive more information or details. Therefore, I wish to assure you that at any time additional information is received it will be transmitted to you without delay, and, if in the meantime no additional information is received, I will again communicate with you at the expiration of three months. Also, it is the policy of the Commanding General of the Army Air Forces upon receipt of the "Missing Air Crew Report" to convey to you any details that might be contained in that report.

The term, "missing in action," is used to indicate that the whereabouts or status of an individual is not immediately known. It is not intended to convey the impression that the case is closed. I wish to emphasize that every effort is exerted continuously to clear up the status of our personnel. Under war conditions this is a difficult task, as you must readily realize. Experience has shown that many persons reported missing in action are subsequently reported as being prisoners of war. However, since we are entirely dependent upon governments with which we are at war to forward this information, the War Department is helpless to expedite these reports.

In order to relieve financial worry on the part of the dependent of military personnel being carried in a missing status, Congress enacted legislation which continues the pay, allowances and allotments of such persons until their status is definitely established.

Permit me to extend to you my heartfelt sympathy during this period of uncertainty.

Sincerely yours,

J.A. Ulio
The Adjutant General

Tracie knew the ladies from Red Cross would soon pay her a visit. They might even bring the dreaded gold star. She would never accept it or the $10,000 insurance money. Doing so would be the same as accepting her son's death, and she would never concede.

Father Orth in St. Paul said a Mass for Dean, at the request of the nuns who loved their mail carrier, Will Tate. Tracie gratefully accepted all the help she could get, even from Catholics. On Thursday, the Newberg newspaper ran a story about Dean on the front page, with the headline, Lt. Dean Tate Reported Missing Over Germany.

Wayne, Will, Tracie, and Dean Tate, May 10, 1942 on
Willamette Street in Newberg, Oregon. Tracie wrote on the back:
"Taken Mother's Day. Dean's last Sunday home."

Newly inducted Dean Tate
in Wichita Falls, Texas,
1942. He would soon begin
a year-long cadet training
program which resulted in
his officer commissioning
and bombardier
assignment.

Dean's original crew of *The Old Fox*. Front row left to right: Sgt. Walter Kelly, Sgt. James Slick, Sgt. Robert Taylor, Sgt. Thomas McCaffrey, Sgt. John Johnson. Back row left to right: Lt. John Martin, Lt. Charles Halfen, Lt. Carl Carden, Lt. Dean Tate, Sgt. George Bishop.

The crew Dean was substituting with on the day they were shot down. Front row left to right: Lt. Eugene Gallagher, Lt. Wright (Dean took his place as bombardier on February 8, 1944), Lt. Bobb Ross, Lt. Williams (Beam took over as pilot with this crew). Back row left to right: Sgt. George Lissandrello, Sgt. William Lessig, Sgt. David Helsel, Sgt. Beyer (Sgt. Robert Kelly took his place as tailgunner on February 8, 1944), Sgt. John Bernier, Sgt. George Fotenakes.

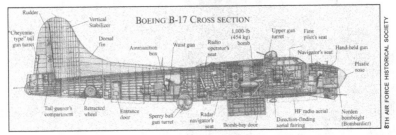

The location of a crew while at their stations in a B-17. Dean sat looking out through the plane's plastic nose, using the Norden bombsight to determine when to drop the bombload.

Dean's B-17 after Lt. Beam crash landed it on a hill above Monchy-Humières, France.

Godelieve Van Laere, 10, stands for a formal portrait in Ghent, Belgium, in 1935, before the Van Laere family moved to France.

Godelieve, age 13, with her nephew Willy on the Fresnières farm where her family worked in 1939.

Godelieve's mother, Martha Van Laere, in the courtyard standing underneath the window of the room where Dean, Bill, and Carl were hidden.

Godelieve was required to carry identification because she was considered a Belgian citizen, despite the fact that she was born in France. Her parents were born in Belgium. When French women voted for the first time in April 1945, Godelieve, without citizenship, was not allowed the privilege. Not until she married would she obtain citizenship and earn the right to vote.

Dean's dog tag, stolen by the guide Maurice in Beauvais, was returned to him in 1991. A Canadian named Tom Lynch had been given the tag by the Resistance because he had lost his and was without identification.

Dean's fake identity card made in Lassigny while he hid at the Van Laeres' home.

Photos taken in a Paris department store for new identification cards. From top left: Dean Tate, Bill Lessig, Everett Stump. Bottom from left: Carlyle Van Selus and Carl Mielke. René Loiseau kept this copy of the photos for sixty-seven years before giving to the author. The writing below the photos is his.

André Duval received the Croix de Guerre for his work as a Resistance agent and hiding Dean Tate, Carl Mielke, Bill Lessig, Carlyle Van Selus and Everett Stump at his home. As a volunteer soldier he stood against the Germans during Hitler's last major offensive at Ardennes, commonly called the Battle of the Bulge, that lasted for six weeks in December 1944 and January 1945.

Twenty-one year old René Loiseau lodged and conveyed about seventy aviators in February and March of 1944, on numerous occasions personally guiding the airmen from Paris to the Brittany Coast for rescue. Dean Tate called him the "bravest man I've ever known."

IDENTITÉ ET SIGNALEMENT

Nom *Rivière*

Prénoms *Jean François*

né le *27 Juin 1915*

à *Compiègne*

Sexe *M*

Fake identification made for Dean in Paris.

Carl Mielke, André Duval, Bill Lessig, and Dean Tate pose for a photo while hidden on the Duval family farm.

Twenty-five years after she helped rescue him in Nazi-occupied France, ex-U.S. flier Carl Mielke plants a thank-you kiss on the cheek of Mme. Jean Pena.

How Do You Thank Someone for Saving Your Life?

by George Barris

PLOUHA, FRANCE.
The first time Ralph Patton of Rochester, N.Y., visited France, he got there by parachute. He dropped from a burning B-17 bomber returning from a U.S. raid on Germany on

Accordingly, the little Brittany village of Plouha was turned into a festive scene as crowds of excited townfolk gathered in the main square to welcome several busloads of equally excited American ex-airmen and their families

"You see," expl Pittsburgher who "many of us barely benefactors. A guided me down pitch blackness. Th

In 1969, Carl and Godelieve met again when thirty-four US and Canadian World War II airmen returned to France for a reunion with dozens of French men and women who helped them after they had been shot down. Carl, intending to propose to Godelieve, found he had waited too long and she had married someone else. Carl never married, having said he couldn't find anyone like Godelieve.

Dean and his daughter Susan in their Portland, Oregon home, 1965.

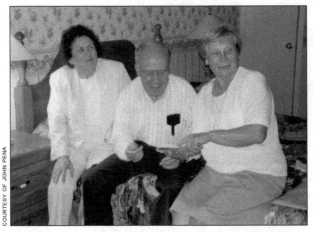

Dean and Godelieve are reunited in San Francisco, 1996.
Left to right: Lillian Tate, Dean Tate, Godelieve Van Laere Pena.

Godelieve and the author attending a ceremony in Le Cardonnois, France, for a crew that was shot down on February 8, 1944. In attendance are family members of the crew, including the widow and daughter of the bombardier who was killed in the plane before it went down. French citizens, like Godelieve, who helped hide airmen, often attend these ceremonies whether they were involved with the particular crew members or not.

TWENTY

SABOTAGE

Dean woke to the unfamiliar sound of birds singing. March had come, and rescue had not. They remained stuck on the wrong side of the Channel while the invasion might begin any day. Over the past weeks, hiding in the barn, Dean watched the others grow listless, bored, and depressed. Thin and emaciated, the five men talked less and slept more. The barn, never warm, had become their prison. Madame Duval, worried about the Americans' boredom as much as their shrinking waists, gave them things to do whenever she could. Today she sent André to the barn with potatoes to peel. When asked, "Any news?" he left with a shake of his head, as he did every morning.

Dean brought his silk map to dinner to discuss ideas with

Monsieur Duval. Van wanted to set out for Paris. Beauvais was over two hours away on foot, and the Channel was another hundred kilometers from there. The entire northern coast was behind barbed wire and heavily patrolled by Germans on high alert anticipating an invasion. They discussed heading south for the Pyrenees, a route Dean knew had been used with a guide, not alone. In the winter it might not even be passable. The Italian border was well guarded and a distance of over a thousand kilometers. It could take months. Last night, after listening to the news, Dean had asked Monsieur Duval about a route to Switzerland. The old man just shook his head and said, "Impossible." All they could do was wait.

By the time Dean got back to Kimbolton, it was possible his crew would have finished their missions and gone home—if they were among the few who survived twenty-five missions. Even now they might be prisoners or dead. The thought of his friend, Mac, dead or imprisoned depressed him into substituting the idea, whenever it cropped up, with thoughts of home and the people he missed. Easter would arrive soon, although he wasn't sure exactly when. Whenever it occurred in early April it might coincide with his or his mother's birthday. Easter had never meant much to him, if he'd ever thought about it at all. The church service bored him. His parents and brother sang in the choir leaving him to sit alone, looking forward to the hot cross buns his mother would serve at home after the service.

But now, his chest ached remembering the Methodist Church on Easter morning smelling of lilies and furniture polish and the way the sun shone through the stained-glass window at the same angle on that day each year. After a lunch of ham and potatoes, his family would pile into the chestnut-colored sedan for a Sunday drive, ambling along country roads and into the hills surrounding Newberg, his mother chattering away and his father driving in silence, his mouth turned up in a contented smile. It was the safest place he could remember, all of them tucked in together.

The men talked to each other, mostly of home, sometimes venting frustrations, making plans they knew couldn't be executed. Bill paced, to keep warm and use his legs. "It seems a waste, ya know? We could be helping to end this thing, but we're just sitting here day after day, useless, while our friends are fighting and dying."

Carl, lying down on his makeshift bed of straw, stared up at nothing as if hypnotized and said, "I used to feel trapped in the tail, like I was the only one on the plane. Sure, I could hear the guys on the interphone, but when we got shot down and the interphone went out, it was just me. This is worse, because it feels like it's never going to end. We're just waiting for the Germans to find us, and they will, sooner or later."

Everett got up and stretched; moving kept body temperatures up. "When Jerries were firing at me during a battle, it felt good being able to fire back. I was too busy to think about dying. Now, that's just about all I think about. Dying in battle is fast; this kind of dying is slow."

Dean worried they were all losing their minds.

Dean woke to Bing barking frantically. Van sprung to his feet and said, "Someone's here." André stepped inside, and he was not alone. A stranger entered the room. Dressed in a white shirt and plaid tie under a dark blue trench coat, he looked like an undercover detective who'd wandered away from London. His dimpled baby face, full lips, and clear blue eyes did nothing to detract from his imposing demeanor. He removed his derby hat and smoothed his thick hair, telling them his name was Jacques du Pac. In his work he went by many names, most often Jacky; his full name was Jacques Henri du Pac de Marsoulies. "I work for British military intelligence." He didn't sound British, or French either. "All I do is eat, make love, and kill Germans." The Americans nodded, unsure if he was serious or joking. "I will need to ask each of you some questions, beginning with the lieutenant."

Dean followed the intelligence officer into the tack room where du Pac settled himself on a stool and took out a cigarette. Dean faced him, waiting, hoping the questions would be straightforward.

"You are in no danger as long as I believe your answers are truthful. If I suspect a lie, you will be a dead man." Dean nodded and took a deep breath to calm his growing terror. "Lieutenant, who plays in the movies with Bob Hope?"

This was not at all a question Dean expected, and he wasn't sure how to answer. He had never been good at remembering actors' names. Sweat began to chill his armpits. Would he be killed over a simple and ridiculous question? Only one name came to mind. Attempting a confident tone, he answered, "Bing Crosby."

Du Pac's slanted eyes surveyed him without expression or indication of whether or not he had given the correct answer. He lit a cigarette, taking his time, as if enjoying the ritual, before continuing. "How many bases in baseball?"

"Three, plus home plate. Four all together."

Du Pac tilted his head to one side, scanning Dean from head to foot. Dean wondered if the agent looked for the twitch of a facial muscle, too much blinking, or some other sign of deceit, and willed himself to relax. "What bomb group are you with?"

"The 379th."

"Where do you live in the United States?"

"Newberg, Oregon." When no response came, Dean continued, "It's a small town about thirty miles from Portland."

"I hear Boston is a beautiful city." Du Pac leaned back and took a long, slow drag from his cigarette, eyeing his victim through the smoke.

"Boston is on the East Coast. Portland, Oregon, is on the West Coast."

Du Pac nodded once, and Dean suspected he knew exactly where the two Portlands were located. "Tell me about your family."

"My father's a mail carrier and my mother does seasonal work at a filbert factory. I have a brother in the Coast Guard stationed on the Oregon Coast."

"And the date you arrived in England?"

"October 14th, 1943."

Du Pac looked skeptical. "You arrived the day after the Schweinfurt battle?" As they talked about the fated battle, about which du Pac seemed fascinated, Dean found he liked and admired the man and began to relax.

Du Pac took a long drag and frowned as if considering something. "Who do you think would make a better president, Bob Hope or Harry Truman?"

"That depends on your politics." Dean regretted the flippant remark as soon as it was spoken. Jacques du Pac had cleverly managed to get him to drop his guard and forget the importance of the interview. The intelligence officer studied him, his cat-like eyes narrowing until they appeared to close, and then he threw back his head and laughed.

"Well, my friends, I am sorry to say that I will not have to kill any of you today," du Pac said after questioning the other airmen individually.

"Do you ever make a mistake?" Dean asked.

"Kill someone who isn't a spy?" He brought his hat to his head. "If I make a mistake and kill the wrong man..." he shrugged, "I answer to no one."

Du Pac told them they would next be taken to Paris before the final journey to the coast. Airmen were not brought to Paris until a rescue was scheduled. Before that time, it was easier to get food in the country.

Du Pac shook his head while inspecting the photographs on their identity cards. "It's as if you have the word 'American' stamped on your foreheads. No matter what we do or what clothes we dress you in, nothing changes that look. In Paris, photos will be taken for new identification, and you'll need work permits and certificates of residency. There are some thirty Americans being hidden in and around Beauvais and another forty near Crèvecœur. We'll get you all back."

He lit another cigarette, offering around a pack of Gauloises bleues. "There are many people in Paris, both French and German. If you're not careful, you'll stick out like a sore thumb. Let me give you some advice. The French don't smile easily with people they don't know. Americans are always smiling. The Parisians will think you make fun of them or are just plain stupid if you walk around smiling all the time. In queues Americans are easy to spot. They leave an arm's length between themselves and others. The French crowd close together."

"Bill, if you smoke like that, you'll be a dead man." Bill studied his cigarette between his index and middle finger. "Like this," Jacques demonstrated, balancing his cigarette between the tips of his index finger and thumb, "with finesse."

He went on, "Americans sprawl casually in a chair and take

up as much space as they possibly can. The French keep their elbows in, and their legs crossed. Do you have your escape kits?" They told him they did. "You don't want to be caught with those. If you have any francs left, you can keep those, nothing else."

"Can we keep our maps?" Carl asked.

"Not if you want to live," du Pac said and stamped out his cigarette.

Two endless days passed after du Pac's visit, and Dean began to wonder if they would spend the rest of the war in France. Dean reports in his Escape and Evasion report, "On March 9, a large number of trains passed through Beauvais moving south and the Beauvais airfield was bombed with excellent result, not like September when most of the bombs fell on the town."

The following day in the late afternoon, André appeared and said, "Is now time you go." They had no belongings to pack. They were ready.

Farewells were brief, taking place in the courtyard between the barn and the house as the light faded in the sky. Monsieur Duval took a dirty rag from the pocket of his coveralls and wiped it all over his tearstained face. The driver, an expressionless man built like a linebacker, loaded them into the back of his truck with no more than a dismissive grunt before closing the tarp. The Duval family stood waving as the old farm truck disappeared from the yard, rattling and coughing like an old man clearing his throat.

As the driver picked up speed, the Americans braced their feet against the floor and held onto the bench and each other as he raced around curves. The French drove the same way they lived, as though they had nothing to lose.

A young man waited in the gathering shadows to receive his first parcels. A Parisian by upbringing, he was not familiar with Beauvais, but he had found the church and the alley behind it easily enough. René Loiseau was twenty years old and on his first mission.

At the age of eighteen, Loiseau joined the French Navy. A year later, in 1941, he was operating an anti-aircraft machine gun in Bizerte, Tunisia. By the time the Allies invaded North Africa in November 1942, the French Navy had been forced to take its orders from the Germans. René, ordered to shoot the Allies, said, "This is not my war." He refused, and was arrested, charged with military degradation, and put in a high-security prison at Menzel Abderrahmane where he endured complete darkness for sixty days.

When he managed to escape, he returned to Paris and lived with his parents again. While he had been away, his mother had become a member of the CND Castille Network, one of the most important Resistance networks in the occupied zone. Madame Loiseau met Jacques du Pac while working with the network, and he in turn recruited René to retrieve downed Allied airmen and transfer them to Paris; dangerous work requiring courage, patience, and acting ability.

In the alley with Loiseau was another man named Alain Fleury. Alain was twenty years old, only a year younger than Loiseau, now twenty-one, but his small size caused the Americans to mistake him for a boy. His father, Georges Fleury, was the mayor of Rémécourt and head of the Resistance in the region of Oise. When René Loiseau arrived at the Fleury home that morning, Alain begged his father for permission to join the trip leading the airmen to Paris. His father finally gave his consent. Helsel and Bernier were being hidden on the Fleury estate and were bitterly disappointed to be left behind.

When the old farm truck turned into the alley, Loiseau stepped into the headlight beam and, lifting his cap, ran a hand through his hair using the signal of recognition. No introductions or words passed between Loiseau and the driver. Anonymity saved lives.

The evaders followed Loiseau a few blocks to the Beauvais train station. Jacques du Pac had briefed them at length on what to do on the train to Paris. "If anyone speaks to you, pretend to be deaf and mute. You may be questioned. Say nothing. Shake your head, look confused, point to your ears as if you cannot hear. Do not follow your guide too closely, and try to go through the entry with a group of people. If you are found to be American, you will be shot."

The instructions left Dean deflated. Acting deaf and mute might not be too hard, but would he be able to continue the act if he was questioned? He felt lucky enough to have traveled by train twice without incident. To do it again without being discovered seemed impossible.

A French police officer was checking identification on the platform, and as Jacques had warned, beside him stood a German disguised in French uniform—a trick Dean hadn't noticed when they came through this station nearly a month ago. The Nazis didn't trust the French police, as there had been incidents when the French had allowed an evader to pass through.

Dean held out his identification, arranging his face into what he hoped was an expression of indifference. He could hear his own heart beating. The Nazi soldier, a pale teenager with bloodshot eyes, took the card and looked at it closely. Dean experienced a swell of compassion for the exhausted-looking boy who waved him on with a disgusted sneer. Having passed, Dean moved forward with the other passengers toward the train.

Loiseau led the five evaders into an open carriage where Dean slid across the wooden banquette making room for the others. A man muttered, "Bonjour," before taking the empty space beside Van and opening his newspaper. Dropping his chin, Dean pretended to sleep. A long, shrill whistle signaled their departure and the train began to move.

When Dean opened his eyes a few minutes later, the guide studied him over his opened newspaper with penetrating blue eyes. He wore the uniform of a French sailor, a short, dark jacket over white wide-legged pants, a white cap sat on the seat beside him. His blond hair, un-parted and slicked back, exposed a broad forehead and long face. He looked too young to be a sailor, and Dean wondered if it was a disguise.

The countryside remained cloaked in long shadows as they thundered toward Paris, closer to rescue and closer to greater danger. Dean's heart beat faster at the thought. If the invasion happened now, they should be safer in Paris than in the north. Hope, and the rhythm of the train, lulled him to sleep.

He woke to a high-pitched squeal and the train coming to an abrupt stop. The lights had gone out, leaving the compartment in darkness. Somewhere outside, angry voices shouted. Something was wrong. Loiseau tilted his head toward the door, and the Americans followed him off the train.

Nazi soldiers stood in a line parallel to the tracks. Their flashlights were held high to light the ground, and the single shaft of light grotesquely illuminated each angular face. Dean wondered if the train had broken down, or if the Nazis were searching for Allied evaders. He knew German soldiers sometimes took French hostages from trains. If the Nazis suspected there were evaders on board, they might question everyone. This idea threatened to paralyze him. He forced his legs to move forward.

The air smelled of creosote and cigarettes. Someone yelled

up ahead and Dean's heart beat heavily in response as he followed the sailor and the crowd along the tracks. The other
passengers clutched one another, stumbling and talking in
hushed, frightened voices, words he couldn't understand as
they followed the path of flashlight beams.

A German voice shouted, telling them to hurry or shut up.
Then Dean saw what had happened: the railroad tracks were
blown apart. One track simply ended, and the other curved
away as if it had decided to go off in another direction. People
whispered and pointed, barely controlling their pride in the
act of sabotage. Stopping the trains, or even slowing them
down, would make it difficult for the Germans to get into, or
out of, northern France, an important precursor to the invasion. Someone had risked his life to do this, someone like
René Buffard or André Duval.

Dean kept moving, watching the ground and wishing he
knew when the invasion was going to happen. It could be
tomorrow or the next day. Looking up, his thoughts were
replaced by a more immediate concern. German soldiers were
forcing everyone to stand side by side in a line facing the
tracks. The sabotaged tracks had created an inconvenience.
They were not pleased.

Dean believed the Nazis might execute some of the gathered people. They could do whatever they wanted and without
provocation. His mind raced and he wondered if he could
duck into the shadows without being seen, but it was too
late—they were watching him. He took his place between a
stranger and Van. Two Nazi soldiers began checking identification, making slow progress, holding their flashlights over
the offered identification before shining a light into each face.
Dean told himself to look inferior, unable to control his shaking. He stood beside four other Americans who had all been
given the same advice: to behave as if they were deaf and

mute. They should have spread out. Terror rushed through his body, hot and cold at the same time.

A soldier questioned a man down the line. Dean would not be able to answer the simplest question. None of them could. His mind screamed at him to run into the darkness. There was no escape. The Nazi soldiers were coming to him next.

Dean winced as the flashlight's beam crossed his face three times before coming to rest on his identification. Willing his hand not to shake, it shook anyway. The soldier took a deep breath and exhaled slowly, a tedious task on a cold night. He studied the card and said something so quietly Dean wondered if he was talking to himself. It didn't sound like a question, but a comment or a complaint, maybe about the circumstances they found themselves enduring. Dean looked into his eyes. The German held his gaze for less than a second, nodded and stepped over to Van. Dean kept the frozen expression on his face. It quickly dissolved when the German spoke.

Van answered without hesitation, "Oui."

Dean's stomach rose in panic. If he threw up, he'd ruin it for everyone. Why was Van speaking French? He was going to get them all killed. The soldier stepped away and stood before Carl.

They were doomed. The moment Dean had feared was happening and he could do nothing. He counted, one, two, three. It was taking too long. Dean turned his head enough to see the soldier had moved on to Everett, whose slightly stupid expression seemed to be working. The Nazis continued on down the line. They had survived. For now.

After a tortuous amount of time, the crowd started to shuffle forward, heads bent to the ground. Dean stayed close to the sailor's back as the darkness became deeper, forcing him to follow the guide's rhythmic footsteps.

For over an hour they followed the tracks like silent refugees, until they came to a dimly lit train station. A sign read, *Creil*. A train stood waiting beside the platform veiled in smoke and hissing. Dean had never been so happy to see a train.

It was two hours past the eleven o'clock curfew when the train finally arrived at the Gare du Nord station in Paris. An announcement informed the passengers the cars would remain heated until morning and they would be allowed to sleep there. The Americans, unable to comprehend the message, looked to Loiseau who was making a place to recline against a window beside the boy. Satisfied with his makeshift bed, he closed his eyes.

After enduring the sabotaged tracks, the scrutiny of the Nazi soldiers, and a long hike, Dean was exhausted. He wanted to stay awake, if possible, to keep an eye on the guide in case he tried to disappear. This time they had no money in a public place with pairs of armed Nazis patrolling the platform, many with dogs ready to kill on command. Du Pac said the Germans were becoming more ruthless under threat of the coming invasion. Defeat was not an option for them.

Loiseau leaned against the cold window glass with his eyes closed. This was the first time he had escorted airmen into Paris, and the sabotaged train tracks had interrupted their timing. Another guide was supposed to have met them there and led the Americans to a hiding place in the city. When the train didn't arrive, the guide would have been forced to leave, if he hadn't been caught. Either way, Loiseau was now stuck with five Allied evaders, and he had no idea where to take them.

All moves were kept strictly secret, so he didn't know where the airmen were to have been taken. He couldn't take them to the basement room under the tobacco shop where cell members met, and Philippe's, a discreet café and meeting place, would be closed so early in the morning. And there were five, far too many to move easily. They would have to be separated, which meant he needed two places to take them—and he didn't have one. In the morning, when curfew ended, he would disembark with five men who looked like Americans pretending to be French. His career was going to be a short one.

TWENTY-ONE

PARIS

At six a.m., Loiseau woke the Americans and led them off the train into the busiest station in Europe, the Gare du Nord. Bright and cavernous, its high ceiling supported by ornate art nouveau columns, it took discipline for the men to avoid looking around like tourists. Long, black trains waited in rows for the whistle to signal their departure. Nazi soldiers with rifles slung across their bodies walked among the crowd.

Dean tried to keep a few people between himself and the guide as he'd been instructed, but the fast-moving crowd made it difficult to find the young sailor. Throngs of people filled the station's concourse. On dimly lit corridor walls, angry red propaganda posters glared at him: Hitler surrounded by swastikas, German soldiers with children, and another warning against associating with *des Juifs*. They took a stairway to an underground platform where the white tiled walls were marked with ominous dark stains, and the stench of urine and sewage permeated the air. The platform began to shudder, and the crowd massed toward the tracks as a commuter train appeared from the tunnel, gliding to a stop. Windows and doors glowed a golden light onto the waiting faces.

Dean boarded and followed the guide down the center aisle. People scattered about the compartment continued reading. Dean, Bill, and Everett sat on wooden planked benches facing each other. Loiseau and Carl sat together in single seats at the rear of the compartment. When the conductor came through, Dean held his ticket between two fingers while holding the newspaper du Pac had given him to cover his face and avoid conversation.

Thirty minutes later, they disembarked at the Pont de Levallois Métro station to find another identification checkpoint standing between them and Paris. Dean watched the guide navigate the identification process and prepared to act deaf and mute.

"Bonjour," the French policeman said, looking at Dean's card. Dean stared forward, expressionless. The tall, blond German soldier said something to the little French officer. They both looked blankly at Dean as if they couldn't remember what he was doing there or as if maybe he knew the answer. Dean's heart pounded so loudly in his ears he feared the two men could see his temple pulsating. He couldn't afford to take a deep breath to calm the shaking. The French officer looked at his watch and answered, "Non," and laughed. The German, looking likewise amused, gave Dean back his identity card and dismissed him with a "Merci." Dean's legs turned to jelly. In an effort to look sober, he strode toward the line of doors at the terminal exit.

Dean emerged from the underground Métro station into a different world. Tall, cream-colored buildings, all with the same neo-classical façade, rose toward a blue sky laced with delicate white contrails. Windows had been thrown open onto small wrought-iron balconies to let in the crisp spring air, and car horns, trucks, and bike bells created an overwhelming clamor. German soldiers, rifles slung across their bodies, walked purposefully on the crowded sidewalks.

Loiseau and Alain led the Americans through the over-crowded workers' district, the 17th arrondissement, one of the most populated neighborhoods in Paris. Tiny green buds clung to the branches of the trees lining the streets. Solemn Parisians hurried past with their heads lowered as the five evaders followed the guide onto Rue Baudin. In the street a group of boys kicked a ball to each other, yelling insults and instructions. The ball rolled to Dean's feet, and he stooped to pick it up. Tossing it back to a thin boy in baggy pants holding his arms out, Dean could not remember ever having been so young.

Loiseau turned under a portico at 5 Rue Baudin, and led the Americans through a courtyard and into an apartment building. Upstairs, on the top floor, he knocked on a door marked 23. A woman answered, smiling at Loiseau as if he were the only person in the world she wanted to see, and then seeing the Americans hanging off to the side, her smile melted. Her name was Marguerite di Giacomo, but she was called Margot. She waved the men inside with a nervous glance down the hallway.

In the cramped entryway of Margot's apartment, the Americans clumped together like awkward schoolboys, peeking into the sitting room, which was flooded with light from floor to ceiling windows. The sailor and the woman spoke briefly, before she turned and introduced herself and Loiseau and

Alain. She was thin, dressed in a vivid green blouse and dark skirt, with dark somber eyes and thick brown hair curled around her shoulders in tumbling waves.

The sailor, named René Loiseau, extended his hand. Dean shook it and smiled at the young man, hoping to convey his gratitude. "Lieutenant Dean Tate. Thank you." Loiseau took Dean's hand and said, "Bon."

"Sergeant Bill Lessig. West Chester, Pennsylvania. Nice to meet ya." Loiseau nodded.

"Sergeant Everett Stump. West Virginia."

"Sergeant Carlyle Van Selus. Portage, Wisconsin."

Carl removed his cap and shook Loiseau's hand. "Sergeant Carl Mielke. Baltimore, Maryland."

Margot said, "My daughter is sick. Typhoid." Van took a step backward and Dean grabbed his arm. "No fear! My friend will help," and she slipped out of the apartment.

Loiseau went to the tall windows and stared out. Yvonne might be able to keep three of the men at the most. As much as he hated to put his parents in danger, he had no other choice. He would have to take two airmen to his own home. He turned to study the Americans still standing in the entry. The tall one looked almost French; he could stay here. His eyes landed on Bill, the most American looking. He'd take him to spare Margot and Yvonne the danger should someone come snooping around, and the lieutenant, because hosting an Allied officer would be an honor to his parents.

Margot returned with another young woman, named Yvonne, with whom the three men would stay. Yvonne Latrace worked as a waitress at a café called Philippe's on Rue Daunou where a back room served as a meeting place for Resistance members. She could stay with the men at her apartment next door during the day until she reported to work.

Loiseau led Dean and Bill across the street to an apartment at 4 Rue Baudin where they found, sitting companionably with an elderly couple, Jacques du Pac. He sprang to his feet, keeping his voice low as neighbors could not be trusted if they heard English being spoken. "My friends! Allow me to present René Loiseau's parents, Alfred and Suzanne Loiseau." René's father, who looked to be in his nineties and blind, stood up and crossed the room slowly with a hand outstretched. Dean met him halfway and grasped the cold, papery hand. The old man offered the only English word he knew, "Good."

Alfred Loiseau, blinded in the First World War, was a broom maker. The bare room indicated making brooms wasn't bringing in much income. Dean knew they would have little, if anything, to share.

When Dean expressed his surprise at finding du Pac in the apartment, du Pac explained that he lived there while in Paris. He used Loiseau's room, and Loiseau, still in hiding, stayed at Margot's. He put his cigarette out in a small dish. "I was just telling Monsieur and Madame Loiseau that the evaders are not showing enough patience—not using their heads by not making contact after they're shot down. We cannot help the airmen if they hide from us."

Dean said, "It's difficult to know who to trust, especially right after being shot down."

"It is the same for us," Jacques spread his hands wide.

Jacques translated for Alain. Two gunners from Dean's crew, David Helsel and John Bernier, were being hidden at his home. Dean was sorry to hear that Alain couldn't have brought them to Paris, too, understanding the boredom and restlessness in waiting. Jacques assured him that they would be brought forward for a future rescue, but numbers must be kept small and returning officers remained a top priority of the network. Dean experienced the familiar guilt associated with being treated differently than other airmen, especially when, in his opinion, gunners were more important during a mission than a bombardier. There wasn't much skill involved in dropping a bomb load.

As they talked, Bill asked if the network had ever been infiltrated. Du Pac told them there were attempts from time to time, usually rendering the compromised line unusable. Six weeks ago the entire network was threatened when a man in Paris claimed to have been shot down but didn't know anything about flying. His story was that he was Norwegian and had sailed to England where he had been making recordings of bombers in action for transmission by the BBC. He had been in an American plane when it was hit. All he knew was the pilot's name. His story didn't check out, and the order was to get rid of him, but he got away. It was later discovered that he had been working for the Gestapo.

Dean wanted Monsieur and Madame Loiseau to know how grateful he was for their hospitality and for the risk they were taking. Du Pac shook his head in protest. "It is nothing. When you return to England, tell them we need machine guns and explosives. From here we would be able to destroy the German factories more accurately than the Allied bombings and without so much loss of life."

Loiseau's mother returned from the kitchen with fried eggs and bread for the airmen and her son, who, like Dean and Bill, had not eaten in the past twenty-four hours. There was a bathroom down the hall, but they could not use it in case someone should see them. An indoor bathroom was a luxury too great to hope for; still, Dean's disappointment sank like a weight into his stomach and he promised himself if he ever got out of France, he'd build a shrine to the first toilet he encountered.

Loiseau told his parents and Jacques du Pac about the

train incident and his concerns about missing the man they were to have met at the Métro station. Jacques confirmed a collaborator had betrayed Loiseau's cell. If the train had not been sabotaged, the Gestapo would have been waiting. Loiseau was in greater danger now. Those in his cell knew his assumed name and might be tortured to reveal him.

Du Pac said, "We will have to do something about your photos. You will need new identification; work permits and certificates of residency to travel into the Forbidden Zone. I'll make the arrangements."

The next morning, Loiseau took Dean and Bill back across the street to Yvonne's apartment. She was small and thin with blonde hair and blue eyes. Her daughters, who were eleven and fourteen, with thick blonde hair like their mother's, ate their eggs silently, seeming indifferent to the strange men eating beside them. Dean wondered if they were used to sharing meals with Allied evaders.

"I worry for them," Yvonne said after the girls had gone to their room. "The penalty for helping the Allies is posted all over the city, imprisonment or death. People disappear all too often. Sometimes their children are taken or left to fend for themselves." She continued talking in a voice barely above a whisper as she carried bowls into the kitchen. Returning, she untied her apron and hung it over a chair. "Do you know when the invasion will begin?" Dean told her what he knew when he left England, knowing it wasn't the answer she wanted.

The girls left for school, and a long day commenced. Before Yvonne left for work in the afternoon, she told them, "Be quiet; no one must hear you speaking English. Do not make any noise, walk carefully and without your shoes or they will hear you below. If someone knocks on the door, do not answer it. Loiseau or Jacques will knock two times quickly, pause and knock two more times. If you must, go out the window and down the fire escape. Find a place to hide and stay there. We will find you."

An hour later, Margot came to find the Americans draped across chairs, flipping through magazines, or in Carl and Van's case, asleep. The watery cabbage soup and bread she served them tasted worse than any they'd had so far. Food had become an obsession, something they craved more than any other luxury, including freedom. After spending the day with nothing to eat, speculating about how long it might take to get back to England and the potential dangers involved in another train ride requiring Academy Award–worthy acting, food was a topic they preferred.

After dinner, Dean found Margot in the kitchen smoking a cigarette and staring out the window, wearing a faded yellow blouse tucked into a dark blue skirt with scuffed saddle shoes.

She turned toward him, and he noticed the dark shadows under her eyes. He accepted a cognac and said, "I appreciate what you're doing for us. But I'm concerned for you and your daughter and Yvonne and her girls. I think it might be better if we went somewhere else."

"There is nowhere else." She tapped her cigarette into the sink. "The French are used to being occupied, you know. It is in our blood. In 1914 there was more chaos, terrible looting and destruction, so we thought maybe it would be better this time." She shrugged. "It began peacefully enough. We laughed when we read the posters telling us to *have confidence in the German soldier*."

"I don't understand. Why take the risk to help us? I mean, what's in it for you?"

"Freedom, of course. We want you back in England dropping bombs on Germany." Her small smile quickly faded. "Cigarette?"

"No, thank you."

She bit her lower lip, as if debating whether or not to say any more. "I have not seen my husband in four years. He was a jeweler. We don't receive letters. I don't know if I will ever see him again. Maybe he is dead." She looked into his eyes and Dean found himself wanting to look away.

"We nearly starved when the Germans came and the bombings kept up for two days. Nearly everyone left Paris. Even though we had nowhere to go, we joined the Parisians on the roads heading south. It was a horror I will never forget. And then, unable to find food or a place to stay, we were forced to return home." Her eyes filled with tears and she turned away from him to lean on the sink for support.

Dean didn't know what to say. He wasn't used to older women baring their souls to him. Margot and Yvonne seemed willing to sacrifice everything, even their children, to defeat those who had taken away their life and freedom. He didn't know how to respond, and whatever he said would be lacking. To change the subject he asked, "Have you hidden airmen before?"

She crushed her finished cigarette into a saucer. "No, this is the first time. Loiseau was desperate. You were supposed to have been met at the train by someone, another guide, but when your train was late, he was forced to leave, and René didn't know want to do. He didn't want to bring you here. He is overprotective; I hope now I will be able to help more in this way." She blew a plume of smoke at the ceiling and smiled.

"Do you know Jacques du Pac?"

"Yes, he was recently promoted and given control of the Oise line in northern France. Because he can speak English, as well as German and French, without an accent, he interrogates aviators. He is important, although not as important as he thinks he is." Dean followed her into the next room where the others sat looking at magazines. She lit a lamp and watched it sputter to life while Dean looked down into the courtyard from the window.

"Is he French?"

She closed the shutters and pulled the drapes across the windows. "He was born in Saigon. His parents were French, I believe. How long since you are shot down?"

"Over a month. We were shot down February eighth," Dean told her.

Rummaging through a drawer, she made a sympathetic sound and said, "I hope you will be home soon."

Margot spread a map on the table and the men gathered closer to see. "This," she pointed, "is our apartment. And this is the Loiseau's apartment across the street." Then she pointed to a building a few blocks away. "Here is the Jaeger watch factory where I work. This building across from the factory is a warehouse with a red roof and blue skylights. Easy to see from the sky, yes?" She looked at Dean. "Will you remember?"

"Yes," Dean said, unsure what she wanted.

"When you get back to England tell them about the factory where I work. It is important to the Germans. The parts we make are vital to their airplanes. Tell them about it, and they can bomb it."

Dean shook his head. "I understand what you're telling us, but I won't tell anyone about this factory."

"You must!" Her eyes opened wide. "No one suspects, because we are a watch factory, that we make parts for Germans planes." She turned her pale face to the other men and pointed to the map. "Tell them when you return. If you have to, bomb the factory with me in it."

The others could do whatever they wanted when they got back to England, but Dean would not tell anyone about the factory. Margot stepped up to Dean and for a minute he thought she was going to kiss him. Instead she whispered, "Please, tell them."

From the door came two knocks followed by two soft taps. Margot opened it and Jacques du Pac walked in followed by Loiseau and Alain.

"What is this?" he asked, spotting the map laid open on the table.

Margot folded the map and returned it to the kitchen. Dean guessed she wasn't sure she could trust Jacques du Pac. When she returned carrying two wine bottles and glasses, she wore a bright smile, eager to lighten the mood. "Old people say we won the First War thanks to wine and applejack. We may starve, but we always have something to drink."

Jacques raised his glass. "Tomorrow, my friends, you will have your photographs taken. You will pretend to be Parisians. God help you."

The Paris department store, Au Printemps, rose from the Boulevard Hausmann like a palace. Dean gazed up at its majestic façade; an opulent, wrought-iron structure embellished with elaborate mosaics and ornate gilding. Parisians hurrying along the wide sidewalks looked exhausted and sunken. They kept their heads down, as if wanting to be invisible, and didn't seem to notice the rain, or the Americans walking among them.

Dodging bikes and a delivery truck, Dean crossed the boulevard and followed Loiseau through the main doors into a spacious courtyard smelling like jasmine and citrus fruits. The jeweled dome several stories above had been dismantled to preserve it from air attacks. The main floor resembled a ballroom crowded with glass-cased counters displaying jewelry, perfume, scarves, and cosmetics.

At one counter, a black-clad SS agent flirted with a salesgirl. Seeing him, Loiseau skirted the main floor and led the Americans toward a dramatic staircase, which split halfway up before spiraling to the second floor. Dean kept his head down, questioning Loiseau's wisdom of parading them on the staircase, where they could be seen from anywhere on the floor below.

The photographer was a small, nervous-looking man. His usual subjects were children, much safer customers than Allied evaders. He did not look happy; no one in Paris looked happy. Margot had given the men haircuts before she left for work this morning, and Loiseau brought new clothes for them to wear: suits and ties for Dean and David, black jackets over sweaters for Bill and Van, and a dark jacket for Carl that threatened to completely engulf him.

Without saying a word, the photographer gestured Dean into his booth with a small bow. He whispered, "No smile, please." The entire process was completed in less than ten minutes, and the group quickly exited out a back door.

Dean kept his gaze downward until they reached the steps descending below ground to the Métro. On the platform he was pushed directly behind a German soldier, the dagger at his waist close enough for Dean to reach out and touch. He withdrew to avoid bumping into the man, before he remembered what du Pac had said about the French standing close together in crowds. Stepping forward, Dean noticed the soldier smelled of freshly cut limes, and his mouth watered for a gin and tonic.

When they exited the Pont de Levallois Métro station, shutters were being drawn as the Parisians performed their nightly blackout ritual. Nazis poured into cafés, while citizens scurried home to prepare their meager meals. Dean held his arms close to his body, all the while being careful not to smile. It wasn't easy. Smiling at people on the street came naturally to Americans.

Later in the evening, Jacques du Pac, Loiseau, and Alain returned to Yvonne's apartment with two young women. While Everett played a clumsy melody on a piano, the brunette sat down beside Dean. She smoothed her flared black skirt and adjusted a thin red belt she wore over a gray cashmere sweater. Her dark hair was styled into waves and her lips were blood red, and a white scarf tied in a knot at her throat trailed down between her breasts. When she asked Dean if he spoke French, he told her he didn't. André and his family had picked up English quickly; the Americans somehow managed to learn almost no French.

After telling him her name was Marcelle, she suggested Dean join her for a short walk outside. The offer to feel the fresh air, to be immersed in the innocent normalcy of walking with a girl, was too much to refuse. They had made it to Paris, Dean reasoned. Loiseau and du Pac would get them to their rescue destination, and today in the city they had easily slipped past Nazi soldiers undetected. The attention of the beautiful young woman made him feel inextinguishable.

"Sure," he said, flashing a smile.

"Shoo-er," she mimicked, with a laugh.

Margot noticed Dean helping Marcelle into her coat and said in English, "Curfew is in one hour." Marcelle said something to Margot in French. Margot would not be persuaded. "Have you forgotten the girl shot for speaking English with the American airman? He was taken prisoner while she bled to death on the sidewalk. It is too dangerous." Marcelle closed the door on Margot's protests.

Paris, nearly deserted so close to curfew, spread before them. Without gaslight, another wartime casualty, its buildings and cobblestone streets were washed in blue. Dean and Marcelle walked arm in arm until they came to a wide tree-lined boulevard. On the other side, the Seine was a black expanse betrayed only by its stench and the intermittent caress of water against its banks. Tentatively, Dean and Marcelle crossed the vacant boulevard to walk in silence along the river, exhilarated by the rare freedom.

"There is no fun in Paris anymore," she said in a whisper. "The boys are all gone, and dances are forbidden by the Germans." Dean wished she wouldn't talk—someone might hear them. After a few blocks, she pulled his arm to lead him back across the street. A German lorry, its headlights blacked out, rumbled up the boulevard like an old dog coming home after a day out hunting. They pressed against a building hoping to disappear into it. His heart beat furiously, and he could feel her body trembling.

She probably weighed less than a hundred pounds. In the States he would take her out for a hamburger and French fries and apple pie slathered in rich vanilla ice cream. His hunger made the memory painful. This was a different kind of hunger. He missed the experience of food and the feeling of contentment and happiness that surrounded a satisfying meal shared with friends or family.

A few steps more brought them to an alley. It appeared unoccupied so they turned into it, walking close to the buildings, skirting the moonlit wedge flowing down the cobblestones. He could feel her warm shoulder, and the scent of an exotic flower floated up from her hair. She told him she was studying to be a singer. Nearly tone deaf, he had to fake his way through the Air Corps song whenever singing it was required, and, worse, he could never remember the words.

She stopped, her face lost in the shadows, and he felt her finger trace a line along his jaw as she leaned forward to kiss him. For a brief moment, he remembered the boy he'd been before he was drafted. With her lips pressed to his, she stepped closer. As she did, her foot caught something, and a thunderous metal clatter echoed up and down the alley.

She fell into his chest, shaking. The garbage can lid at her feet continued to rattle a decrescendo until it fell silent while they stood frozen against each other, hearts beating out the seconds, listening.

"Let's go back," he whispered into her hair. He felt her head bob up and down. Surely everyone for miles around had heard the crash, and it was after curfew by now. He cursed his stupidity as they walked back to the apartment.

Later that night, Dean lay awake in bed listening to a faint sound grow louder until he recognized it: plane engines. He waited for the air raid sirens.

Bill whispered, "I didn't hear a siren."

Dean went to the window and scanned the black sky. Bursts of anti-aircraft fire echoed against the buildings, and a muffled explosion rumbled somewhere in the distance. He had been twenty-one thousand feet in the air when he released the bomb loads. Now he understood the terror people experienced when a formation approached, ready to obliterate its target.

"What's their target, do you think?" Bill asked.

"Probably the railroads."

"Think we'll make it out before the invasion?"

Dean didn't answer. Sirens screamed on their way to a casualty. He lay down and pulled the covers around him for warmth. There would be no rescues during the invasion.

TWENTY-TWO

THE FORBIDDEN ZONE

Early Wednesday morning, March 15, a man in a meticulously tailored suit arrived at Yvonne's apartment. He spoke English well, having lived in Canada for twelve years and in the United States for two. Born in France, he returned at the age of fourteen. After his wife's death, he resigned from his executive position at Ford Motor Company to work full-time with Reseau François, becoming chief under Paul Campinchi, the head of the organization. Reseau François was the name given to the rescue operation in Paris which gathered downed Allied airmen, feeding and lodging them until the time they could be sent to Brittany. He told the Americans his name was Yvon.

An envelope stuffed inside his capacious fur-lined trench

coat held false identity cards, work permits, and certificates of residence that would allow the American airmen to pass into the Forbidden Zone on the northern French coast of Brittany along the Channel coastline where travel was restricted and more heavily guarded by Germans. Dean's new identity card and papers identified him as Jean François Riviére, a twenty-eight-year-old single craftsman from Compiègne. Each of the Americans was given the name of a person who lived or had lived in the Côtes du Nord region where the airmen were heading.

Jacques inspected the new photographs like a proud father and said, "Now you look almost French!"

A radiant spring morning flooded the Rue Anatole with sunlight, and an unseasonably warm breeze stirred the chestnut trees ready to burst into leaf. The five American evaders tromped along the sidewalk behind Loiseau, elated, after five weeks in France, to finally be leaving Paris on a train bound for the Brittany Coast—and what they hoped would be rescue.

Inside the Pont de Levallois Métro Station from which they had disembarked four days ago, Dean and his comrades endured another tense inspection by a French and German police officer, this time without incident.

Their first stop was less than thirty minutes away, the Montparnasse Station, where Yvon had warned they would be more carefully checked before boarding a train for the Forbidden Zone. As they exited the train, a man in the crowd turned and walked beside Dean. His name was Henri Bois, a former schoolteacher now in charge of the network guides. He discreetly passed the Americans their train tickets, supplied by a French Railways employee named Monsieur Bernard. Behind him were two teenage boys who would guide the evaders to their next destination.

Loiseau gave Dean a small smile before he casually saun-
tered away. His part played, the evaders were now in the
hands of the Shelburn Escape Network. Dean took his place
in line and watched René Loiseau disappear into the crowd.
They had spoken few words in their limited ability with each
other's languages, but Dean would never forget him. He had
never seen any fear in the young man, and knew he had found
a lifelong hero.

The checkpoint line was long at the Montparnasse Station.
Carl, his cap pulled low over his forehead to cover his blond
hair, as Margot had suggested, held out his papers. The Nazi
officer bent down to look at his face and waved him through.
Everett stepped up to be inspected next. He bent his shoulders forward to diminish his height and still towered over the
two officers. Several times they looked up from the papers to
Everett's face. When his papers were returned, he walked
toward the stairs.

Van was next. His examination proceeded quickly, and he
was waved on. Bill's papers fluttered in his shaking hand. His
face remained passive, uninterested, as sweat dripped from
his forehead into his eyes. Dean stood beside him, waiting,
sweating, heart racing. After what seemed an eternity, Bill
was waved on.

"Bonjour," one of the officers said. Dean stared forward,
locking his eyes on a distant wall. A muscle in his cheek
twitched. "Papiers?" Dean felt the contents of his stomach
rise as he held out his papers, which were examined and returned with a clipped, "Merci."

The railroad employee who had arranged their tickets reserved a private compartment with room for eight. The
upholstered banquette seats, dark wood, brass doorknobs,
and burgundy velveteen drapes gave the impression of a formal office. Dean collapsed against the window and glanced

toward the doorway where two Nazi officers had stopped to talk. Dean leaned his forehead against the glass and closed his eyes, clasping his shaking hands tightly in his lap. If the two men entered, a simple greeting would unveil them and it would be over; everyone's work and sacrifice would have been for nothing.

When the train lurched forward, Dean partially opened an eye toward the doorway. They were gone.

"Bonjour. Billets?" Dean reached across Carl and handed his ticket to the conductor whose eyes narrowed as he surveyed the disheveled group. "Vous allez à la côte du nord?" The guide sitting nearest the door answered him, and he disappeared with a soft, "Merci."

Dean retreated into silence. The train raced through a pastoral countryside like a muted pastel painting under filtered afternoon sunlight. White cows bent their heads to brilliant green grass near a stucco grain silo, as the sun sank in the western sky. Heading west toward freedom, the speed of the train reminded him of flying, and a new hope burned in his core. Maybe within a week he'd be home.

He recalled something the vicar had said to him. *If we can die with our hearts and minds fixed on attaining an honorable goal, knowing we have lived out our purpose regardless of our personal success or failure, then we have lived a life that matters.* At the time, the words sounded lofty and confusing. His goal to get home, to comfort his parents by letting them know he survived, had become secondary to a bigger purpose. The war had become more than a politician's war to him.

Godelieve and everyone who had risked their lives to get him to rescue were living lives that mattered, regardless of whether they succeeded or failed; hearts and minds fixed on the honorable goal of freedom. He hadn't helped or made any difference; instead, others had made a difference to him. He wouldn't be able to go back to living the isolated life he'd created before being shot down. The suffering and injustices he experienced in France belonged to him, too.

His reflection in the window startled him. He needed a shave. Sunken cheeks and eyes, huge and somber, stared back. The face looked older than he remembered. He didn't feel old, just incredibly alive. What would happen next seemed impossible to guess, and he found he didn't care much. After coming this far, the rest of the journey didn't intimidate him. He lifted his chin in greeting to the new man, a new version of who he had once hoped to become.

Dean snapped awake. Everett was shaking him and whispering urgently, "They're leaving us here." His head tilted toward the teenagers waiting in the corridor outside the compartment. "We have to catch another train." One of the guides motioned frantically for them to get moving. Everett pulled out his francs and handed them to the boys who grinned and vanished out the door. The Americans were on their own.

A sign posted on the station read, *Saint-Brieuc*. Everett led the way along the platform, following the crowd. They passed train compartments filled with Nazi soldiers staring languidly from filthy windows. German troops had abandoned military trains because civilian trains were less likely to be bombed or strafed by Allied aircraft. At the last car, soldiers stood guard beside a flat wagon with a turntable and four forty-millimeter machine guns.

Dean tucked his chin into his coat and continued following the slow-moving crowd to another platform where a line had formed, and at its front two police officers stood questioning a man about his papers. The next person in line, a woman, was questioned, too. Dean heard her answering. He looked around wondering if they could leave the line or whether that would draw too much attention. Everett turned and their eyes met. This time they had no guide to help them.

A couple watched them with pale, anxious faces before stepping forward. They knew. Five men walking away from the line would be suspicious. Margot warned them about German police in civilian clothes watching for people who left the line.

Dean decided if asked a question, he would not answer. He would pretend to be deaf and mute. After taking a deep breath he forced his face into a blank expression, determined to make no reaction to anything said to him. When it was his turn, each of the two officers carefully looked at his papers and identity card. Dean stared at a fixed point beyond them, opening his mouth slightly and letting his eyelids droop enough to look unintelligent but not drunk. His papers returned, Dean continued to walk away in character, shuffling his feet, hoping he had given his last performance.

The five evaders boarded a small commuter train, having been told to get off at the next stop and look for a man in a gray fedora who would be there to meet them. In fifteen minutes, they pulled into the station at Châtelaudren. Twenty-two evading airmen had come through this station over the past three days. Eight, including Dean's group, the final group, passed through in the past few hours. The tiny station, a kilometer south of the village center, was deserted except for two French police stationed to see visitors' special papers needed to disembark at this station within the restricted coastal zone.

The lack of a crowd to meld into caused the airmen to feel exposed in a new way. They showed the papers Yvon had provided and kept their heads down.

After passing through the inspection, they were met by a man in a gray fedora. Mathurin Branchoux, a forty-seven-year-old, broad-shouldered potato merchant, carried himself with the rigid forbearance of an English gentleman. Though Brittany had long been part of France, its residents considered themselves Briton first and French second. Branchoux's job as head of the Guingamp Armée Secrète resistance group was to receive parcels—or in his case, they were called "a sack of potatoes"—at the station and arrange lodgings where the men would be hidden, usually at local farms, until they were called forward to the coast.

Dean, Carl, Bill, Van, and Everett followed their new guide on the Rue de la Gare through the outskirts of the tiny village called Plouagat. Once outside the village limits, they walked into a thick wooded area for some concealment since it was still daylight. After a distance of about three miles, they came into a village and approached a school and a small stone church. Children played in the yard and when they saw the men, they stopped, staring, and grew quiet. One by one, as if instructed by some unseen authority, they turned back to their game.

Branchoux would have preferred another hiding place for the evaders—a church and adjoining school were too public— but he had no choice. The evaders had arrived "rewrapped and stamped," meaning dressed and equipped with identity papers, and had been easy to spot as they stepped from the train, ambling forward in their casual American gait and looking like film stars.

Branchoux led them to the back of the church where he pulled open the double wooden doors to a garage built underneath the church building. Assorted tools hung over a workbench, and an ancient car had found its final resting place.

As the doors closed behind them, the children's voices muted, the light disappeared, and the garage became colder and more tomb-like. Dean thought of the children outside, concerned for their safety with Allied airmen hiding nearby, and envisioned them being questioned by Nazi police. His fear was interrupted by the garage doors opening again, flooding their faces with light.

A large man ducked into the garage, introducing himself only as Claude. He was followed by an older, Napoleon-like character who gave his name as Captain Harrison. They were both British Intelligence Officers. Their true identities were Raymond LaBrosse and Lucien Dumais, the two men responsible for establishing the northern Shelburn escape route which had become known in operation as Bonaparte.

An interrogation commenced, led by LaBrosse. "You entered the country by parachute?"

"Yes, my plane was shot down during an attack," Dean answered.

LaBrosse leaned back against the car. "I've parachuted into this country many times. One time I was holding a bicycle wrapped around each arm." Dean stared at him in disbelief. Maybe the man was testing his gullibility. LaBrosse grinned, turning his cheeks into parentheses. "I needed the bicycles for transportation."

He asked about the circumstance of their journeys, and the five men told their stories of being shot down and rescued, fumbling through the details because so much had happened.

"You're lucky to have made it to this point. The southern escape route through the Pyrenees is more difficult. I took that route about a year ago with twenty-seven airmen after we were nearly caught. We made it by some miracle."

After the interrogation they were told to wait until tomorrow night. They tried to sleep, but ended up pacing, trying to get warm. At times they heard someone outside. By nightfall hunger replaced apathy, and each man lapsed into his own thoughts. Dean remembered the words of the older intelligence officer: "This is a new route, recently established, and only used twice." The thought of a barely proven route kept him awake, uneasy, and wishing there were some other way.

TWENTY-THREE

THE ESCAPE ROUTE IS CLOSED

Canadians Lucien Dumais and Ray LaBrosse left the evaders in the church that afternoon with optimism for the planned rescue operation the following night. After arriving at Guingamp that morning, the two men noticed the Germans patrolling the streets in trucks with equipment inside to detect radio signals. Despite the increased German presence, they believed all would go well, and the following night a third group of allied airmen would be safely returned to England.

The Germans had captured Lucien Dumais—a tough, thirty-eight-year-old platoon sergeant in the Canadian Army—during the ill-fated Dieppe invasion in 1942. He and several other POWs managed to escape and return to England. In November of 1943, after months of combat training with the British First Army in North Africa and bored with the routine of army life, he asked to return to France as a secret agent to help others escape as he had. And so, his path crossed with that of another Canadian named Ray LaBrosse.

Ray LaBrosse first went overseas in 1940 at the age of 18 as a signalman with the Royal Canadian Corps of Signals. The British secret service agencies were chronically short of good wireless radio operators, especially those fluent in French, and MI9 asked him to become their first Canadian agent. His first mission into German-occupied France ended abruptly when the Gestapo infiltrated the network and LaBrosse was forced to flee the country.

In February 1943, LaBrosse parachuted into France to organize a sea escape route, but when his partner was arrested, he and a group of twenty-seven airmen he'd collected were forced to escape to Spain. After that, he was eager to get back to France and renew his efforts. LaBrosse had qualities that suited him well as a spy: outstanding courage and good sense, combined with a quiet and calm nature. He proved to be an excellent partner for the forceful, tough, and articulate Dumais.

In November 1943, Dumais and his radio operator LaBrosse, under the direction of MI9 in London, were secretly dropped into France to organize an escape network that would return downed Allied airmen to England. The two men had undergone intensive training in everything from jiu-jitsu to building and operating wireless radio sets. Equipped with pens that fired tear gas, buttons concealing hidden compasses, large amounts of francs, and forged identity papers, Dumais and LaBrosse set up what would become the most successful escape network of World War II: the Shelburn Escape Line.

After interrogating the five airmen in the church garage,

Dumais contacted François Le Cornec, a Resistance member who owned a café in Plouha. Le Cornec told them the entire coastline had been put on alert; no one knew why. All boats and water vessels were to be confined to their ports under guard. The rescue planned for the following night would have to be canceled.

A flat tire kept the two men from reaching Plouha on time. LaBrosse left immediately for Paris by train. In the meantime, Dumais investigated the alert and found that only senior German officers knew the reason, meaning it must be credible.

The following evening, March 16, as Dean and the others waited in the church garage, Lucien Dumais paced the worn floor of Le Cornec's café in Plouha. It was there that he and LaBrosse had first made plans for code name "Bonaparte," the Shelburn network's escape-by-sea operation.

Because the first two Bonaparte missions on January 24 and February 27 had run smoothly, and successfully returned 29 Allies to England, Dumais decided to try three evacuations during the next moonless period. The route proved an excellent path to freedom and Dumais didn't want to lose it. Now he sat with Le Cornec in his café listening anxiously to the radio for a code that would tell him whether or not LaBrosse had been successful in canceling the rescue. A program on the BBC called *Les français parlent aux français, the French speak to the French,* was forbidden to the French population who listened to it anyway. After each program came personal messages, which were actually disguised instructions to Resistance networks in France. The Germans tried to mask the messages with interference, so Dumais listened carefully with his ear bent to the radio. At seven p.m., the message came over the BBC. "Bonjour, tout le monde a la Maison d'Alphonse!" *Hello to everyone in the House of Alphonse.*

The message told Dumais that a Royal Navy gunboat was

ready to leave Dartmouth and would arrive off the Brittany coast later that night. LaBrosse had not been able to cancel that night's rescue.

With a cargo of parcels awaiting shipment and a gunboat on its way, there was no choice but to proceed. Lives were at stake if the gunboat was left waiting in the Channel. He dispersed the guides to quickly round up the airmen. Dumais hoped it was not a trap. At nine, he returned to the café to wait for the confirmation message. Following the nine o'clock news, again they heard, "Bonjour, tout le monde a la Maison d'Alphonse!" This second message meant the gunboat had already left England. There was no going back.

TWENTY-FOUR

THE HOUSE OF ALPHONSE

Spring twilight lingered long after sunset. Everyone involved in the impending rescue waited for complete darkness. At ten-fifteen, an hour after Dumais received the final message from England, an old farm truck driven by François Kérambrun pulled up outside the garage doors behind the church. Kérambrun owned a garage in Guingamp and carried supplies for the Germans during the day. At night he carried evading Allies to their final destination, a cottage on the coast called the House of Alphonse.

François pulled back the canvas flap and Dean climbed into the truck while the exhaust pipe grumbled softly. He could just barely make out the forms of other men. Their teeth glowed in the darkness as they scooted along the bench to make room for the new additions. In less than thirty minutes Kérambrun came to a stop and opened the tarp for the men to scramble out. Without a second wasted, Kérambrun, his part played, drove away.

A sailor named Jean Gicquel had offered his home—the stone cottage where he lived with his wife, Marie, and new-born baby girl—as the rendezvous point for the Bonaparte rescue operations, and in so doing it was given a name much grander than its appearance: the House of Alphonse. It rested less than a mile from a beach tucked into a rugged coastline of rocky outcroppings and hidden coves.

When planning the rescue missions, Lucien Dumais believed the beach called Anse Cochat would be an ideal location for rescues, as long as the evaders could navigate the hundred-foot collapsed rockfall down to the beach in absolute darkness.

It was after eleven when Dean, Everett, Carl, Bill, and Van arrived. Twenty-two Americans and one British airman filled the main room and adjoining kitchen. Like the Van Laere home, the two rooms were separated by a corridor in the middle. Jackets and sweaters hung from their bodies, eyes and cheeks sunk into dark hollows, and pants sagged from their withered waists. Several lifted their heads and smiled to welcome the new group, acknowledging the miracle that had brought them to this final stopover on the long route back to England. The silence felt like hiding in wait at a surprise party, with the same mood of electric anticipation.

Marie Gicquel waved her hand at Dean and pointed to an open space at the table. He smiled back at her and sat down. This young woman, barely more than a girl, holding a baby in one arm, deserved rescue, not him. Ashamed, he lowered his head to the cabbage soup.

The other men took turns crowding around the kitchen

table. Excited about their rescue, they flirted with Marie, flashing white teeth from dirty faces. Most had not bathed or showered in weeks, some for months.

The door opened and fresh sea air rushed in as several newcomers stepped into the cramped room. Dressed as peasants, these people had made the Resistance their profession. Dean's confidence rose. If anyone could pull off a difficult rescue and evade the Germans while doing it, it would be these people. The leader, sporting a well-groomed mustache and a determined expression, was one of the two men who had come to interrogate them in the church garage. Unknown to any of the evaders, he was Lucien Dumais, the mastermind behind the night's rescue mission.

Dumais addressed the airmen in English. On his list were twenty-two names; twenty-four evaders, two more than expected, were inside the house. Spies would be easily found out and disposed of. Nervous fidgeting ensued; but no one came forward. Dumais consulted a list and spoke with a woman who pointed out two men standing by a blacked-out window. Dumais walked over to them and demanded their names.

"Lieutenant Kenneth Ralph Patton, sir."

"Lieutenant Jack McGough. We were shot down on January 4th over Brittany and have been hiding for two and a half months."

"Where were you stationed in England?"

Patton answered, "Bury Saint Edmunds, sir."

"Where was your last stopping point when you left the USA?"

"Wait a minute!" someone shouted. "You don't have to answer those questions. You're an officer in the US Air Corps—give him only your name, rank, and serial number."

"Shut up!" Dumais screamed like a man possessed. The

room fell silent. "I'm Captain Harrison, British military intelligence. It is my job to get you back to England. Some of you may have a hole in your belly, but you'll get back." He pointed his forty-five at the men standing around the room who shrunk back against the walls.

Turning back to the wide-eyed Americans in doubt, he lowered his gun and said, "You two answered too poorly to be spies," and leafed through papers handed to him. "Patton and McGough, you're on my list for the next operation. You were brought early. That's okay. You will join the others going back to England tonight."

With the same authority and cool command Dean had admired in Colonel Preston, Dumais turned and addressed the men. "Well, fellows, this is the last lap of a long journey, but the most dangerous one. We are about a mile from the Channel; if everything goes well, you'll be aboard a British warship in two hours and in England by nine o'clock in the morning." The men smiled at each other and made subdued happy noises in lieu of cheers.

"When the guides get ready to leave, you will form up in single file. Each one will hold on to the coat tail of the man in front. There's no moon, and if you don't hang on you'll lose sight of the man you are following. If you do lose him, stand still and make no noise; the guides will straighten you out.

"When you reach the coast, you'll have to go down a steep cliff. Lie on your backs and slide down. When you get to the bottom you'll be told where to sit.

"There will be no smoking, talking, or coughing, either on the way or on the beach. Small boats will come in to pick you up. When ordered to, and not before, you will wade out to the boats and get in."

Dean felt a chill of terror. He didn't know how to swim. His brother had tried to teach him many times and failed.

"If we're attacked, you are all expected to fight. Some of the guides have pistols, but if you have a knife, use it. If not, use your hands, your feet, or your teeth. If you get your hands on somebody, make sure it's a German, and then show what you can do."

"If you get lost, any farmer in the vicinity will help you, and you only risk going to a POW camp. Do not say anything about this set-up. Your guide is risking his life and that of his family, so give him a chance. Any questions?"

He looked around the room at the disheveled crew waiting for further instructions, trusting him to return them to safety, and said, "Goodbye, and good luck."

TWENTY-FIVE

"THEY'RE FIRING AT US!"

Dean, Carl, Bill, Everett, and Van stood in darkness, waiting.
It was one a.m., and their group would be second to depart.
The lead guide, Jean Huet, opened the door to take the first
group out in single file. A seventeen-year-old named
Marie-Thérèse Le Calvez led Dean and his group out next. A
local farmer named Jean Tréhiou, along with Clement Huet
and Le Cornec, led the remaining groups. Dumais brought up
the rear with Job Mainguy, a retired naval captain whose
Morse code signals would guide the rescue boats to the beach.

Dean reached out his hand until it found Everett's shoulder. Each slow, unsteady step was like plunging off a cliff into
oblivion. Thick vegetation growing along the narrow path
grabbed his legs and feet. The line moved steadily, if slowly,

until his feet splashed into a black stream of water. Falling into the bank on the other side, he stepped up and found Everett waiting for him.

A twig snapped and a whisper followed, "This way." The air, damp and chill, held the encouraging scent of the sea.

The path climbed to the headland, where they left the trees and the wind picked up. Tumbling waves echoed from below as Dean looked upon the vast blackness of what must be the Channel. White caps, like sea creatures, raised their frothy heads, and he shivered. Across the dark abyss was England. That he could be so close to the Channel, within walking distance, terrorized and intoxicated him.

Marie-Thérèse pushed on his shoulder; Dean sat on the ground with his legs around Everett, and Van did the same behind him. As a train they scooted down the steep, serpentine path on their backs, digging their hands into the dirt to slow their descent. Near the bottom, rocks loosened by those still coming down the cliff fell in a shower on their heads. Dean jumped the last few feet onto the beach and followed Everett and Marie-Thérèse to a rocky outcropping jutting out toward the sea. There behind the rock wall, they would be protected from the Germans' searchlights at Pointe de la Tour less than a mile to the northwest. Sitting beside Everett, Dean carefully leaned his back against the jagged rocks as Carl, Bill, and Van joined them.

The water hissed onto the beach a few yards away. No rescue boat appeared visible in the black sea. Dean worried this tiny indentation in the coast could be easily missed. And they were trapped between the water and the insurmountable cliff.

Dumais, waiting at the water's edge, stared into the dark expanse and switched on his walkie-talkie. When he heard, "Dinan," the code word meaning the gunboat was about four miles offshore, he answered, "Saint-Brieuc." The evacuees squatting on the sand with their backs to the cliff began to whisper excitedly. Marie-Thérèse drew her knife and held it toward them, effectively stopping the chatter.

Dumais signaled to Le Cornec to get the men ready as the sky over the water lit up, followed by a loud explosion. The Germans from the nearby lookout were firing toward the Channel. Another shot followed.

"Holy Jesus, they're firing at us!" someone said.

"Shut up!" Dumais hissed, holding his ear to the transceiver.

From the walkie-talkie came, "We're being fired at. We'll have to pull out for the time being, but we'll be back."

Three more explosions shattered the silence, each reflecting light onto the men's faces. Dean sat frozen against the rock wall, his mind racing with questions. Did the Germans know they were hiding on the beach? Would they be captured, or would the Nazis simply open fire on the cove, killing them all? He dropped his head onto his knees. He did not want to die here on this beach after coming so far.

Silence settled into the cove. There was nothing to do but wait. "The gunboat was not hit," Dumais reported over his shoulder.

Someone asked in a strained whisper, "Do you think they'll be back?"

"They'll be back," Dumais answered, but he knew in a few hours, daylight would expose the twenty-four Allied evaders pushed up against the rocks. Dumais had promised himself to evacuate every Allied personnel stranded in France. He would not accept defeat on only his third operation, especially with another rescue planned in a few days.

Two hours passed. Dean's back began to spasm and cramp. He rubbed his legs and then his hands and shifted his back against the jagged rock face, searching for a position that wasn't agonizing. Dumais remained standing, holding the walkie-talkie to his ear. He spoke the password again as he had been doing every ten minutes. This time, "Saint-Brieuc," came the reply. "Any trouble ashore?"

"None," Dumais answered. "How about you?"

"We're on our way back."

"Any damage?"

"No. We should be ashore in half an hour."

The British gunboat 502 of the 15th Motor Gun Boat Flotilla, British Royal Navy, under the command of Peter Williams, worked her way between German patrol boats to drop anchor less than three miles offshore next to a rock called Le Taureau, the Bull, where German radar would be unable to detect the ship. The anchor was noiselessly lowered by hand into the choppy sea. Radar systems had difficulty distinguishing between sea swells and small ships, making the gusty weather an unexpectedly opportune condition for the operation.

Job Mainguy, squatting halfway down the cliff along the serpentine path, began to signal the Morse code letter "B" with a masked flashlight every two minutes. Down on the beach, Marie-Thérèse flashed a blue-screened light continuously. The two signals in alignment would guide the rowboats to the precise location in the cove where the Allied evaders waited.

The boats first appeared like black phantoms silently gliding toward shore, where high tide allowed them to come deep into the cove onto a sliver of beach. Dean wondered if he was imagining the sight, if his hope had become a vision. Five wooden skiffs, each with two oarsmen holding them steady, rose and fell in the black water. One slid gracefully onto the sand, and Patrick Windham-Wright—the British liaison officer responsible for beach rescues—approached the group of French guides gathered to meet him. In minutes, heavy suitcases filled with weapons and ammunition were unloaded to the French operators. At low tide, the heavy bags would be carried along the narrow beach to a road.

The evaders, having been directed into single-file lines, waited to enter the water, aware that the beach was covered by mounted machine guns ready to shoot them as they boarded the skiffs. Dean's feet disappeared and the force of the sea tugged at his ankles. The thick water rose to his knees, pulling him down. The certainty of drowning threatened to immobilize him. No time to think about it. In two steps he could no longer lift his legs against the numbing cold. Holding his arms out for balance, he plodded toward the boat. Another step. Any deeper and the water would swallow him.

Arms reached out to grab him, pulling until he slid into the skiff, breathless and weak from exhaustion and terror. "All here?" someone asked.

Dean raised his head and saw his four friends sprawled on the boat's bottom.

"All here," he answered.

Dean curled into a fetal position, wet and shivering. Despite the cover of darkness, the Nazi guards on the nearby cliffs would surely see their movements or hear them and open fire. The boat rose and fell, rocking him painfully against the floor while the rhythmic slap of oars urgently pressed them out to deeper water. The steady beat became the rhythm of his mantra. *We have to make it.*

The oars fell silent, and the boat dipped and rose like a roller coaster. Someone was throwing up. Dean opened his eyes. Overhead, the stars reached their arms toward one another. Someone told him, or he had read, that the stars always glow brightest before dawn. Dawn was the enemy now.

The searchlight dominating Baie de Bréhec from Pointe de la Tour could have exposed the entire operation. A 76mm cannon mounted at this location threatened the total destruction of everyone there.

And then the gentle purr of a motor drifted on the water like a lullaby.

Dean's fingers were too cold to grasp the rope ladder leading up to the gunboat. A hand reached down and lifted him as if he weighed no more than a feather, and a blanket was placed around his shoulders. "Welcome aboard, sir. You're safe now."

Dean grasped the railing and looked back toward France. A yellow light and smaller blue and green lights flickered on the cliffs where the German lookouts were posted. They would be seen, hidden only by fading darkness that would soon give way to morning. Getting the men aboard was taking too much precious time. He counted to forty before the motor grew louder and the boat moved, turning in a gentle arc toward England.

Why the Germans fired that night would always remain a mystery.

The gunboat surged toward Dartmouth under ever-brightening cirrostratus clouds. Dean was handed a warm cup. He put his nose to it and inhaled. Coffee. Sipping it, he found someone had even added cream and sugar.

The pink sunrise spread across the eastern horizon and above it a single star hung in defiance against the dawn. Carl, also wrapped in a blanket and holding a steaming cup, came and stood beside him. His face reflected the orange glow of the rising sun, and he smiled. Dean wrapped an arm around the young sergeant and together they watched England's shoreline draw closer.

TWENTY-SIX

LONDON

The British gunboat 502 docked at Dartmouth Harbor and the twenty-three men were transferred to the HMS Westward, a warship that served as base for the 15th Flotilla of the Royal Navy. They were taken to a lower deck and welcomed home by the captain. Dean was examined by a ship physician and allowed a hot shower. He couldn't remember the last time he'd had a shower, hot or cold. He was given a British uniform and, after they had been made presentable, the men sat down to a delicious hot meal of roast beef, potatoes, and apple pie.

Dean boarded a train for transport back to London with Bill, Carl, Everett, and Van. Spirits were high and the big meal had left them tired and content, but once on the train, they were separated and put in guarded and locked compartments. Uncomfortable being alone after so much time spent among others, his exhaustion won out and he slept.

Exiting the train, he was asked his name and handed over to a British Intelligence Officer who took him to a waiting car. They drove past Hyde Park, where barrage balloons flew garishly over the shells of bombed-out buildings and piles of bricks and rubble. The car stopped in front of a brick residence at 63 Brook Street. Dean was put into a single room, again locked and guarded. Until someone came to identify him, he was essentially a prisoner. He arrived with no identification other than one dog tag, which he could have stolen or purchased. Until proven otherwise, he would be considered a possible spy. He slept soundly until someone woke him later in the day.

The American Intelligence Services offices, including the office in charge of the Shelburn Escape Network, were located in an aging Victorian hotel. Hours of questioning and paperwork began in a small office with an intelligence officer and a secretary. Dean was asked to tell the officer everything he could remember from takeoff on February 8th to his delivery back to England. The secretary wrote down his words, asking questions when needed. He was asked the names of the people who had helped him in France and the names of the towns and villages where they had hid.

The interrogation continued for three days. He was asked where German airfields were located and where soldiers were billeted, and anything else he saw or heard while escaping. He explained that much of what he had heard was hearsay and communication mostly by word of mouth, and therefore possibly unreliable. Remembering the details of his journey exactly as it happened was difficult, and he knew they would compare his story with the others. In between sessions he was not allowed to call or write to anyone, not even his parents.

He was asked about the factory in Paris on the second day, and he knew one of the others had told them. "Yes, there's a factory near the apartment where we stayed. French civilians work there." They showed him a sketch one of the others had drawn. "I hope you won't do anything about this information. The woman who hid us and risked her life to do so works there. That would seem a poor way to thank her." The factory was never bombed, and Margot went on to hide more escaping airmen.

Questionnaires and various forms were completed and signed. Finally, the officer told him not to discuss the details of his escape with anyone. "We do not want to jeopardize these routes for the airmen still trapped in enemy-occupied countries. If you are asked to lecture to airmen about escape and evasion, the particulars will be clearly given to you. In general, though, you can say you were shot down over enemy territory and you escaped. Period. An exception, of course, is high-ranking officials." Then he passed across the table several pages to be signed. At the top of each page in red were the words *Top Secret*. "Signing this document means you are under oath to keep secret your escape experience, specifically the names and places, for fifty years. Please read it carefully."

Dean said, "I want to know what happened to the rest of the crew I was shot down with, besides Bill Lessig and me. We only heard rumors in France." A piece of paper listed the crewmembers' names, each paired with a handwritten acronym: POW, KIA, or EVD. Helsel and Bernier had not returned, but a penciled note said they were due with the next rescue. Five had been captured, including the pilot and the tail gunner, Robert Kelly. The priest had been right: the copilot, Bobb Ross, had been killed in action. Dean continued to stare at the paper long after everyone else had left the room, as if the typed words might help him understand what had happened to the men. It all seemed long ago and impossible to comprehend.

He was issued a new American uniform, back pay, and a pass for his time in London until he received further orders. When questioning was complete, the officer stood and shook Dean's hand. "I know I said it before, but again I'd like to say welcome home and good luck."

"Thank you. I need to get a message to my parents and let them know I'm okay."

"Someone will be coming from your base to formally identify you as soon as possible. After that you'll be released from Intelligence Services and allowed to send a telegram. That's procedure."

"Could you send a telegram for me?" Dean laid a five-dollar bill on the table. The officer hesitated a moment before taking the bill. "Tell them I'm well and having a great time."

An hour later, Tony Zaladonis entered the room. Dean stood and shook his friend's hand. "It's not that I'm not happy to see you, but I thought they might send someone from my crew."

"Your crew finished. They left to go home yesterday, all except John Martin. He re-enlisted."

Tracie Tate watched the Western Union courier approach the front door. She had been looking out the living room window to see if it was raining when he appeared. Her blood turned to ice. She opened the door slowly and her eyes met those of the young man holding a telegram in his hand.

"Mrs. Tate?" he asked.

The young man had kind, brown eyes, like Dean's. Will appeared from the kitchen and, reaching her side, held out a hand for the telegram.

MARCH 21, 1944

MR AND MRS W F TATE
WILLAMETTE ST NEWBERG, OR

DEAR FOLKS: HAVING A GREAT TIME. I
AM WELL. SEE YOU SOON. LOVE, DEAN
TATE

"He's safe!" Tracie sang out. Tears spilled down Will's cheeks and onto his sagging sweater. Tracie kissed and hugged her husband, unable to restrain a laugh. "He's safe."

From London, Dean was sent to Dunlap Castle in Ireland. There he spent several months telling his escape and evasion story to incoming airmen who would invade France on D-Day. Dean felt lucky to avoid assignment to the Pacific Theater, for the time being. After rest and recuperation leave, medical and physical rehabilitation, and further training, airmen who made it back to England were sent to the Pacific Theater, because they knew information about the Resistance and its members that would be valuable to the Nazis should they be shot down again and captured. With an invasion looming, Dean was kept in Ireland to continue lecturing on conditions behind enemy lines. He asked to make a trip home, but there was not enough time before the invasion. There were airmen who needed to hear about Dean's experience in case they found themselves in the same situation.

Dean often left base and walked the country roads to find a farmhouse with a sign out front offering a large home-cooked breakfast. Sharing these meals with friendly Irish families eased his longing for home. He found Ireland's verdant landscape rejuvenating, and he discovered teaching suited him. Talking about his experience in France became a cathartic exercise. His future assignment with the Air Corps would be determined after he'd received a medical clearance in the States. Dean feared he would be sent to the Pacific, but for now, he could rest.

In May, he was allowed to go home.

The phone pulsed a busy signal. Depositing more money into the phone, Dean dialed Nap's Grocery. He was about to hang up when his father's quiet voice said, "Hello? Nap's."

"Hi, Pop!" There was a long silence and Dean thought they'd been disconnected, but then he heard his father sobbing. "I'm in New York, at Grand Central Station. I'll be home Wednesday, Pop. I love you. Tell Mom I love her, too."

The train compartment was warm and filled with the sweet vanilla cherry scent of tobacco. Having visited his family and friends, Dean was returning to Texas, where his military career had begun over two years ago. Two years seemed like a lifetime. Soon he'd receive his final retirement papers, granting him an honorable discharge due to disability. Several surgeries had failed to resolve the pain in his back caused by the parachute landing. Until then he would fulfill his orders as a bombardier instructor, safely away from the Pacific.

After the invasion of France in June 1944, the war raged on as the Allies forged their way across France and Germany to Berlin. Nazi Germany surrendered on May 8, 1945, almost a year after the D-Day invasion. With the surrender of Japan, the Second World War ended on September 2, 1945. Dean was released from active duty on December 25, 1945.

She sat on the aisle seat, a porcelain-like face framed by dark curls. Dean strolled up and down the aisle to get a better look. After he walked past, she opened her compact, pretending to check her lipstick, and watched him lean against the doorframe at the back of the car, resplendent in his officer's uniform.

He took another stroll through the car, as if he had nowhere in the world to go, which, he hadn't. This time as he came back up the aisle, he caught her eye and paused. "It's awfully warm for that," she said, bobbing her chin toward his pipe.

"It keeps me cool," Dean answered with a smile and an insouciant shrug.

An unfamiliar feeling came over him, like waking up from a long sleep: he was young and alive, free to do whatever he wanted. Law school didn't interest him anymore. He was twenty-five years old and ready to start living his own life. He had never considered a career in education, but he began to think seriously about teaching as he had grown to enjoy his time as a bombardier instructor. After having spent so long worrying if he would live to see the next morning, the future at last bloomed before him.

Martin had once wondered what it was all about: the war, the sacrificial deaths, the unending terror. Maybe it all wasn't as senseless as it seemed. Ordinary people had sacrificed everything for him and for their freedom. Inspired by the heroism of a young woman thousands of miles away, Dean was ready to commit himself to helping others—whatever that might look like, whatever that might take.

With new confidence and hope, he sat down beside my mother and asked, "Where you headed?"

TWENTY-SEVEN

"FOR COURAGE IN THE CAUSE OF FREEDOM"

FRANCE, MAY 2011

I stand in a churchyard untouched by time under a blue sky dusted with clouds. Viscount Roland du Pontavice, the mayor of this village, reads a speech he prepared about my father. "Le Lieutenant Dean Tate a atterri là," he begins, pointing to the ground just a few feet away. He has been gone seven years, but I can feel the familiar weight of his hand on my shoulder.

Behind me, Godelieve leans on her husband and translates for me, "Your father landed there." She is regal in a white pantsuit and billowing red scarf with gossamer hair in a short bob framing her round face.

Dressed in gray slacks and a robin's-egg-blue sweater like Dad wore in retirement, the viscount's wispy hair blows in the wind like a white flag. This village was forced to surrender to

Germany in the First World War when the viscount's royal father and parents were forced from their chateau. The mayor reads his father's recorded memories from the day an American airman landed in his village.

After the small ceremony, Viscount du Pontavice and his wife, Maxence, serve us champagne and salmon pâté smeared on bread before guiding us through the nearby remains of the family chateau complete with a dry moat.

An hour later, we drive across the countryside with Godelieve behind the wheel of her new Mercedes. Her husband, sitting beside her, yells out directions: "Madame Pena! Allez à droite!" He turns in his seat to smile at me, and from his face, Dad's eyes meet mine. Godelieve married a man with the same eyes as the young bombardier she found hidden in the straw.

I grasp the door handle as Godelieve speeds down the small country roads. She narrates our tour, barely slowing down to point to something. "There is the Calvary where we met M'sieur Vincent before picking up your father," she says as she points to a blur outside the window. Between landmarks she tells me her family had to wait six months to hear any news from the American airmen they had harbored in their home. Soon after the United States Army liberated their village on September 3, 1944, Godelieve learned from an American pilot that Dean, Carl, and Bill had made it back to England. She smiles into the rearview mirror to catch my eye. "That was the best day of my life."

While working for the American Red Cross making donuts for American servicemen, she learned to speak English, but she says she doesn't use it as often now and she's afraid I won't understand her. I assure her that mostly I do, and I apologize again for my terrible French. She waves her hand at my self-consciousness and returns to her memories.

Godelieve corresponded through letters with Dean, Bill, and Carl after the war. When the letters from Bill stopped, she assumed he passed away. I tell Godelieve that Carl never married, and that when he met my father at a 379th reunion he said he had never found anyone like Godelieve. Studying the road ahead, she says, "I never knew that."

We stop at the house Godelieve lived in while Dad, Bill, and Carl stayed with her in 1944. She explains that she doesn't know the new occupants, so we can't go inside. Standing outside the courtyard, she points to the window above the front door and says, "Your father's room." Her husband yells and we turn to see the Mercedes is creeping backward. Godelieve didn't set the brake. Unfazed, she hops in and stops the car which thankfully wasn't moving very fast.

Back in the car, Godelieve slows in front of a brick building that looks indistinguishable from all the others lining the road. "There is the prison where they put my father during the time of chaos after D-Day." We learn that her father rode his bike to Belgium to check on family there, but on his way was arrested by a group of young boys who stopped him at gunpoint. Because he didn't speak French, they accused him of being German and put him in jail. At the prison, Godelieve's attempt to free her father was met with laughter. She waited outside all afternoon until an officer of the French Air Force arrived. She showed him a letter from Canadian Bernard Armstrong, who stayed with the Van Laeres for four months after being shot down and wounded during the summer of 1944. Her father was freed.

I ask what happened to her family after the war, and she sighs. Victory was bittersweet for the Van Laeres. Because they had done business with the Germans and their daughter lived with a Nazi officer, their French neighbors turned against them and they fled to Belgium. Clarisse hid in

Germany with her German officer until years later when she felt safe joining her family in Belgium. Cancer ended her life in 1956.

Later, Edmond Robert's son-in-law, Clermont Jules, welcomes us into the kitchen where Dad met Carl Mielke on their first night in France. The door from Carl's plane hung in their barn for fifty years before Godelieve's son took it to a museum in the United States. The house appears unchanged, and it's like stepping back in time. Monsieur Jules brings out homemade champagne and rips open a bag of potato chips with hands gnarled from hard work and blackened by dirt too long embedded to wash away. Madame Jules wears a smock over a worn dress. She was a little girl when the airmen stayed at her house. It was her father who guided the men to his home, the farmhouse down the road, and the bunker. She places her hands on her heart with tears in her eyes when it's time to say goodbye.

We pull up to a windowless aluminum warehouse too modern to date back to the war. "I'll show you the endive!" Godelieve tells us, leading us inside the building to a dark, refrigerated room lined with carts of small endive sprouts. After the liberation, when the Van Laeres were able to return to France, Godelieve, her brother Jan, and her parents began growing endive. In time, they turned it into a lucrative enterprise. Godelieve wraps her arm through her husband's and says, "He was the delivery driver. He took the endive to Paris." She is actually blushing, telling us how she fell in love with the young delivery truck driver named Jean Pena. They married and raised three children, John, Patricia, and Christine, in a home not far from where she watched a young American lieutenant fall from the sky.

*   *   *

The following days, our journey continues across northern France in homes and at ceremonies where my husband and I are treated as though we personally liberated France almost seventy years ago. André Duval's three grown children yell, "Susanna!" when they spot me with Godelieve in a crowd at a ceremony in a tiny village called Le Cardonnois. They greet me with open arms and wide smiles. Each resembles André in a different way. They show me photos of the five evaders standing in the pasture behind the family farm. Their father never told them about his brave exploits and is now gone. Lung cancer killed many the war could not.

As a volunteer soldier with the French Army, André stood against the Germans when they launched their last attack in December 1944, at Ardennes. In September 1945, he was awarded the Croix de Guerre with Citation to the Brigade for his work in hiding the five American airmen.

André's father Maurice Duval wrote a letter to Dean's parents after the men departed his home, but it did not reach them until 1948. Although Tracie Tate promptly wrote back asking what the Duval family needed, and continued sending them food and other items long after the war ended, the letter was not translated until 2011.

Dears Mr and Mrs Tate,

I have had the honor and privilege of caring for your son these past eighteen days. I keep from your dear Dean an unforgettable memory. Indeed, I kept him, if we could express it in those terms, or more likely hid during eighteen days along with four other friends.

He was so correct and kind. Certainly during his stay with us he didn't get all the modern comfort but with such circumstances, I had to be careful, act with caution, because the least mistake could have been fatal. How many residents have been deported in internment camps and unfortunately did not come back....

Your dear Dean did not ignore that, that's why we could be all together only at night around nine o'clock with my wife and my three children. We could talk together, as with good will we could find a way to understand each other. After hearing the London news release, the Lieutenant Dean gave a signal that it was time to go to bed and all his friends, all very nice, too, followed him out in silence. Maybe he will tell you this story.

It was mostly André my eldest child who looked after them during the day by giving them everything they needed.

We know what you have sacrificed for us. We deeply thank you. You will always have good friends in France,

Maurice Duval

René Loiseau is also present at the ceremony, a handsome, dignified gentleman in a suit the color of a summer sky. After kissing both my cheeks, he apologizes through his son for never having learned English. Like Godelieve, he is in his eighties and remembers my father and their brief shared adventure the way those blessed with age can recall times long past. With pride he shows me a photograph of his family, his beautiful wife and two adult sons. He pulls a piece of paper from inside his jacket. The faces of Dean, Bill, Carl, Van, and Everett, their photographs taken in a Paris department store, stare back at me across time.

After hearing René's story, I ask him if he would consider writing his memoir. A humble man, he tells me he doesn't have a gift for writing. So many stories lost forever.

In 1946, René received a letter of recommendation for

financial reimbursement from the United States stating, "Under ever-difficult and dangerous conditions he fulfilled his missions with greatest courage. In November 1942 he refused to fire on Allies. He helped, lodged, and conveyed about seventy aviators in February and March 1944, and on numerous occasions guided a total of thirty-five airmen from Paris to St. Brieuc and Guingamp." My father considered René the bravest man he ever knew. They exchanged letters for over forty years but never saw one another again.

The last word of Jacques du Pac came on February 9, 1945, when Lieutenant Ray LaBrosse called him in for questioning. He wanted a job. He was working with the French Secret Service and would probably go to the Far East soon; but in case he did not go east, he would like to do some liaison work with the Americans. He had lost most of his personal belongings in a fire and was without resources. LaBrosse recommended him for financial assistance. After du Pac parachuted behind enemy lines into Indochina with other secret agents, many of whom were killed, René heard no more about him.

By the time Margot Di Giacomo's husband was freed from prison in Germany and returned to Paris, she had hidden at least thirty-six Allied airmen in her small apartment and personally guided six Allied evaders across German lines to safety. Like André Duval, she was awarded the Croix de Guerre for assisting downed airmen and was one of few women awarded the King's Medal for Courage at the British Embassy in Paris, as well as the United States Medal of Freedom with bronze palm.

The Shelburn Escape Network never lost one Allied evader in its six nighttime rescues. No airman, Allied personnel, agent, or helper involved with the network died or was captured by the Gestapo. It is the only escape line the Nazis never infiltrated. Seven Bonaparte rescues were carried out between January and July 1944, during which time ninety-four American airmen and thirty-two British and Commonwealth servicemen were rescued and returned home.

The beach called Anse Cochat was renamed Bonaparte Beach for the name given to the motor gunboat operations believed to have been the largest and most successful in France's history. Its success, attributed to the leadership of LaBrosse and Dumais, is also due in large part to the discipline of everyone involved. The citizens involved in the rescues were forbidden to talk or meet, and they hardly knew each other. Every operation was set in motion by the radio. Marie Gicquel said neither her parents nor in-laws knew what she and her husband were doing, and all of the operatives were afraid of Dumais. If someone made a mistake, they knew he would not hesitate to kill them.

The only casualty the Shelburn network suffered was the home of Jean and Marie Gicquel, the House of Alphonse. On July 24, 1944, the Germans, who suspected it was a Resistance hideout, burned down the house after a failed raid that resulted in the Germans shooting one of their own men in the groin. Jean and Marie Gicquel and their baby girl escaped unharmed, and the Allied airmen hiding in the house fled to a nearby wheat field to be rescued off the beach later that night in what was to be the last Bonaparte operation.

At last, I stand on Bonaparte Beach. One hundred and thirty-five men were ultimately rescued here thanks to the countless men and women coordinated under the Shelburn network. Every year on June 7, the local schoolchildren gather on the sand holding photographs of the Allied evaders and release one balloon for each rescued airman, my father included. Today, ours are the only footprints in the sand.

The sun peeks through cumulus clouds hurrying across a pale sky, and the Channel is frothy with white caps. Cold water crawls upon the sand. I shiver, imagining Dad's terror at facing his final adversary: the sea. I was never able to teach him to swim. Beyond the waves I see the phantom image of a wooden skiff carrying the five evaders, growing smaller as the promise of dawn spreads across the waiting horizon.

A few days earlier, I am at Godelieve's home eating tiny iced cakes. Her husband bends down to kiss her cheek and she laughs with abandon. It is Mother's Day in France. Godelieve's two daughters, two grandsons, Jan's son Eric, and Jan's wife Ginette, join us at the large dining room table. Godelieve's brother Jan Van Laere died in March 2002.

"To think," Eric says to me, "if your father had not survived, you wouldn't be here." The truth is, my parents adopted me at birth, and I don't correct him because he's right. I wouldn't be here had Dad not survived. He wouldn't have adopted me, and I'd be somewhere else, a different person without his life entwined with mine.

Before we leave Godelieve's home, she hands me a notepad covered in stains. It's a simple lined pad of paper, each page filled with Godelieve's familiar and unusual script. "I wrote in this journal during the war. The Nazis never found it. Now you must write the story. My children have no interest, and I am too old." Her eyes shine with an intensity that does not appear to have diminished since they first locked onto an unlucky airman so many years ago. I run my hand over the notebook's brittle yellowed pages. "The American boys saved us with no thought for themselves. Future generations should know. We must rely on each other. Tell them we are stronger together."

She grins impishly.

"Tell them."

ENDNOTES

CHAPTER ONE
FEBRUARY 8, 1944

5.   Sincerely friend, Godelieve Van Laere: Letter from Godelieve Van Laere to Dean Tate, January 17, 1945.

7.   peace for every country. Godelieve Van Laere Pena: Letter from Godelieve Van Laere Pena to Susan Tate Ankeny, February 23, 2010.

CHAPTER TWO
THE END OF A DREAM

14. I'll call you when I can. Love, Dean: Letter from Dean Tate, May 29, 1942.

15. proud of you. Love, Mom and Pop: Letter from Tracie Huntington Tate, June 10, 1942.

20. REPORT TO STATION 117: Papers of John R. Martin. Courtesy of Barbara Martin.

21. polar bears playing on one: Journal of John R. Martin. Courtesy of Barbara Martin.

24. good shooting, and good bombing: McLaughlin, J. Kemp. *The Mighty Eighth in WWII: A Memoir*. August 2000, University Press of Kentucky, p. 100.

CHAPTER THREE:
GERMANY

27. good bombing: Journal of John R. Martin. Courtesy of Barbara Martin.

CHAPTER FOUR:
"SOMETIMES, DEAN, I WONDER
WHAT IT'S ALL ABOUT"

34. however well chosen, sound real: Journal of Dean W. Tate.
36. a life that matters: Dean W. Tate, "A Tribute to a Gallant Few."

CHAPTER NINE:
INTERROGATED

70. death shall have no dominion: Dylan Thomas, "And death shall have no dominion," 1933.

CHAPTER TEN:
A BOY NAMED CARL

76. probably a POW. Love, John: Letters of John R. Martin. Courtesy of Barbara Martin.

CHAPTER ELEVEN:
A WORLD WAR I BUNKER

81. had a car: Carl Mielke's Escape and Evasion Report, March 18, 1944.

CHAPTER EIGHTEEN:
NO END IN SIGHT

144. THE ADJUNCT GENERAL: Telegram from War Department, 25 February 1944.

146. Wrote to him: Journals of Tracie Huntington Tate.

148. Sincerely yours, J.A. Ulio: Letter from War Department, 28 February 1944, Major J.A. Ulio, Adjutant General.

149. Lt. Dean Tate Reported Missing Over Germany: *The Newberg Graphic*, 2 March 1944.

CHAPTER TWENTY:
SABOTAGE

157. fell on the town: Dean Tate's Escape and Evasion Report, March 18, 1944.

CHAPTER TWENTY-FIVE:
"FOR COURAGE IN THE CAUSE OF FREEDOM"

220. You will always have good friends in France, Maurice Duval: Letter from Maurice Duval to Will and Tracie Tate.

ACKNOWLEDGMENTS

During the ten years I spent researching and writing the intertwining stories of Godelieve Van Laere and my father, it was a privilege to meet people from all over the United States, Canada, England, and France who came from all walks of life and political and religious persuasions. The diverse group of people who helped make this book a reality showed me what Godelieve meant when she said, "We are stronger together."

I owe a huge debt of gratitude to John Pena, son of Godelieve Van Laere and Jean Pena; Corinne Duval, daughter of André Duval; Christian Loiseau, son of René Loiseau; Roland du Pontavice, mayor of Plessis-de-Roye; Ann Cozad, John Martin's daughter; Linzee Crowe, Barbara Martin's daughter; Nancy and Dennis Scovill; John Kupsick; Dr. Vivian Rogers-Price at the National Museum of the Mighty Eighth Air Force; Anne Marek and Debra Kujawa at the 8th Air Force Historical Society; the airmen of the 379th Bomb Group who shared their stories with me; and Dominique Lecomte who works tirelessly to preserve the history of Allied airmen who were shot down in northern France while uniting their families with the French helpers who hid them.

Thank you to early readers: Randy and Julie Satterwhite, Jeffrey Showell, Daphne Plaut, Teresa Squires Osborne, Patricia Ferguson-Steger, Paul Steger, Tom Titus, Diane Walworth, Mike Maxfield, David McFarlane, John Goff, Mari Partenheimer, Roberta Badger-Cain, Amy Houchen, Greg Moore, and Dick Morgan.

For making my dream a reality, a special thank you goes to my agent Jennifer Weis at the Ross Yoon Agency, and to Marc Greenawalt and Keith Wallman at Diversion Books for their generous and on-point editorial advice.

Finally, my heartfelt gratitude to an invaluable support team: Julie Satterwhite, Sally Woodcock, Betsy Blank, Peggy Paul, Mary Jo Chapman, Beth Enos, Maureen O'Donnell, Diane Gariety, Paula Kurshner, Aimee Ankeny, Emily Chuinard, Charline Ankeny, and especially my husband Joel Ankeny for his patient "bird by bird" encouragement.

BIBLIOGRAPHY

Bendiner, Elmer. *The Fall of Fortresses*. Canada: Academic Press Canada Limited, 1980.

Dumais, Lucien. *The Man Who Went Back*. Great Britain: Hazel Watson & Viney Ltd, 1974.

Ford, Daniel. *Remembering Bluie West One: The Arctic Airfield That Helped Win the Second World War.* Australia: Warbirds Books, 2014.

Huguen, Roger and Rolland Savidan. *Passeurs De L'Ombre: La Résistance en Bretagne avec le Réseau D'Evasion (Smugglers of the Shadow)*. Cinémathèque De Bretagne, 2010.

Huguen, Roger. "Par les Nuits les Plus Longues: Réseaux d'evasion d'aviateurs en Bretagne 1940–1944." France: Coop Breizh, 1993.

MacLaren, Roy. *Canadians Behind Enemy Lines, 1939–1945*. Vancouver and London: University of British Columbia Press, 1983, p. 273.

McLaughlin, J. Kemp, Brig. Gen., USAFR (Ret.) *The Mighty Eighth in WWII: A Memoir*. The University Press of Kentucky, 2006.

Patton, Ralph, "The Shelburn Network." In *Air Forces: Escape and Evasion Society*. Paducah, Kentucky: Turner Publishing Co., 1992.

Pitts, Jesse R. *Return to Base: Memoirs of a B-17 Copilot, Kimbolton, England, 1943–1944.* Charlottesville, VA: Howell Press, Inc. 2004.

Robb, Derwyn, D. *Shades of Kimbolton: A Narrative of the 379th Bombardment Group*. San Angelo, Texas: Newsfoto Publishing Co., 1982.

St. John, Philip A. *Bombardier: A History.* Paducah, Kentucky: Turner Publishing Co., 1993.

UNPUBLISHED SOURCES

Note: all of the following may be found in the author's files

CLASSIFIED ESCAPE AND EVASION REPORTS,
Headquarters European Theater of Operation, Military Intelligence Service, United States Government Archives.

www.archives.gov

Tate, Dean W., March 17, 1944.

Lessig, William G., March 17, 1944.

Mielke, Carl W., March 17, 1944.

Stump, Everett E., March 17, 1944.

Van Selus, Carlyle A., March 18, 1944.

Helsel, David G., March 25, 1944.

Bernier, John F., March 25, 1944.

CASUALTY QUESTIONNAIRES, Headquarters European Theater of Operation, Military Intelligence Service. March 25, 1944. Eugene H. Gallagher, George G. Lissandrello.

INDIVIDUAL CASUALTY QUESTIONNAIRE, Headquarters European Theater of Operation, Military Intelligence Service. March 1944. Bobb F. Ross. Source: Doris R. Beam.

REPORT ON CAPTURED AIRCRAFT, Headquarters European Theater of Operation, Military Intelligence Service. March 25, 1944. Sources: John F. Bernier, David G. Helsel.

US Air Force Military Heritage Database: www.8thairforce.com

Tate, Dean W., "A Tribute to a Gallant Few," 1945. Uncompleted memoir, and letters, 1940–2003.

Journal and letters of Godelieve Van Laere Pena, courtesy of Godelieve Van Laere Pena.

Letters and papers of John R. Martin, courtesy of Barbara Martin and Anne Martin Cozad.

Journal of John R. Martin, courtesy of Barbara Martin.

Journals of Tracie Amelia Huntington Tate.

Duval family letters courtesy of Christine Duval.

Lecomte, Dominique. *Tail End Charlie: End of a Mission in the Skies Over Montdidier, France.* 2011.

AUTHOR INTERVIEWS

Godelieve Van Laere Pena (hid Americans in her home) interviews by author, May 20–29 2011, France; letters to Dean Tate and author, January 17, 1945–August 21, 2012.

René Loiseau (Resistance member and guide) interview by author, May 28, 2011, Le Cardonnois, France; letters to Dean Tate and author, 1949–2011.

Dominique Lecomte (contact to the Unites States Defense POW/ MIA Accounting Agency regaring downed airmen in France; president, Association des Sauveteurs d'Aviateurs Alliés-Oise) interview with author, May 28, 2011, Le Cardonnois, France; email exchanges 2010–present.

Nelly Vincent (French "helper") letters to Dean and Tracie Tate, April 29, 1946–1948.

René Buffard (Resistance member) letters to Dean Tate, 1945–1948.

Roland du Pontavice (Mayor, Plessis-de-Roye, France, whose father witnessed Dean's parachute landing) interview by author, May 29, 2011, Plessis-de-Roye, France; letters to author 2011–2012.

Jacques Zemb (French "helper" and witness to B-17 crash in 1944) interviews by Dominque Lecomte, 2012; letters to author 2011–2012.

Claremont Jules (son-in-law of Edmond Robert who guided Dean Tate) interview by author, May 29, 2011, Thiescourt, France.

Hazel Mary Houser (Dean Tate's girlfriend) interview by author, June 10, 2011, Newberg, Oregon.

John Pena (son of Godelieve and Jean Pena) letters and emails to author, 2011–present.

Barbara Martin (wife of Colonel John R. Martin, Dean Tate's pilot) letters to Dean Tate 1989–1996; letters to author, 2012.

Ann Martin Cozad (daughter of John Martin) letter and father's materials to author, March 5, 2013.

Peggy McCaffrey (wife of Sgt. Thomas "Mac" McCaffrey) letters to author, 2012–2014.

Sam Satariano (379th B-17 pilot) interview by author, August 25, 2012, San Diego, California.

Sgt. Jim Miller (airman shot down over France in 1944) interview by author, June 15, 2016, Hillsboro, Oregon.

Walter E. Benjamin (Superintendent Somme American Cemetery & Memorial) interview by author, May 28, 2011, Le Cardonnois, France.

James Peterson (Historic Wendover Airfield Museum, Wendover, Utah) interview by author, October 2013, and subsequent emails.

INDEX

ABOUT THE AUTHOR

SUSAN TATE ANKENY held a career in teaching before re-
turning to her first love, writing. She is a member of the Air
Forces Escape and Evasion Society, the 8th Air Force Histor-
ical Society, the Oregon Chapter 8th Air Force Historical
Society, and the Association des Sauveteurs d'Aviateurs
Alliés-Oise. Having spent the majority of her life living in
Portland, Oregon, she and her husband recently moved to
Camas, Washington. They have a son and a daughter.